THE POWER OF POSITIVE ANECDOTES

THE POWER OF POSITIVE ANECDOTES

Rakesh K. Mittal

Sterling Paperbacks

STERLING PAPERBACKS
An imprint of
Sterling Publishers (P) Ltd.
A-59, Okhla Industrial Area, Phase-II,
New Delhi-110020.
Tel: 26387070, 26386209; Fax: 91-11-26383788
E-mail: mail@sterlingpublishers.com
ghai@nde.vsnl.net.in
www.sterlingpublishers.com

The Power of Positive Anecdotes
© 2009, Rakesh K. Mittal
ISBN 978 81 207 4769 2

All rights are reserved.
No part of this publication may be reproduced, stored in a retrieval system or transmitted, in any form or by any means, mechanical, photocopying, recording or otherwise, without prior written permission of the original publisher.

Printed in India
Printed and Published by Sterling Publishers Pvt. Ltd.,
New Delhi-110 020.

Foreword

It is a pleasure to go through this book, which is a collection of real life experiences of Shri Rakesh K Mittal over a long period of time. The book is not only highly educative, but at the same time is very captivating with its spellbound magic.

Life is not a straight line. It is not a bed of roses. Nor is it a "Mid Summer's Night's Dream". At times, it becomes the "Tempest" or "Winter's Tale" or "As You Like It". The success and failure of an individual lies in his attitude towards life. This book of Shri Mittal's starting from the 'Stone for Brick' story to the last story, 'When We Think Positive', contains a number of small events, which occur in everyday life in the ordinary course of our journey through life. And each one of them conveys a deep message.

Whatever happens in a man's life at any point of time has a deep meaning and design behind it. To an ordinary person engrossed with the pursuit of materialistic life, these happenings may seem to be ordinary and useless. But to a reflective, philosophical, uncontaminated mind, they convey a deep message and meaning of life whereby; one can bring constant improvement in life. There are excellence, ordinariness, sense of purpose, efficiency, concern, cleanliness, sincerity and all other good qualities all around. According to Mr Mittal, with whom nobody can disagree, spirituality is nothing but a combination of all these qualities. The only difference is that you are not aware of these great qualities of life. Greater than the greatest and smaller than the smallest, the ever luminous spirit resides in each one of us. The moment we realise this, we will immediately transform ourselves and realise our true self and the true meaning of life.

Each one of us is an exclusive creation of Nature and there is a purpose behind our creation. Our effort should be to know that purpose and achieve it. "For this, none of us needs to compete with others, and if at all, there is competition, it is with oneself only." This view of Mr Mittal's is unique and rational and will be a constant source of inspiration for self-improvement in life.

"Human nature is essentially the same irrespective of place, language, colour, religion, caste and creed. All want peace and the mad race for material progress is also an effort to achieve the same objective but in the absence of core values, we fail to achieve it." Therefore, the message of this book is to combine ancient wisdom with modern needs, ideas and scientific developments.

Shri Rakesh K Mittal, a senior IAS Officer of the UP cadre, is an embodiment of all simplicities, human dignities and values. He has written a number of books concerning human values and life. He has a style of his own and he writes in a lucid, simple and easily intelligible language. This book, titled *'The Power of Positive Anecdotes'*, is highly interesting and captivating and each incident conveys a deep meaning and message to life. It will be of immense use to anybody who reads this book. I am sure that it will be a source of inspiration for many who would like to bring positive changes in their lives and to those who would want to lead a carefree, caring, compassionate, honest and integrated life in order to transform this world into a world of peace, harmony, tranquility, fraternity and universal brotherhood.

Union Public Service Commission   **Prashanta Kumar Mishra**
Dholpur House, Shahjahan Road
New Delhi – 110089

Blessings

I feel great joy in sharing my views about Shri Rakesh Mittal's new book, *'The Power of Positive Anecdotes'*. I came to know Shri Rakesh Mittal while he was posted in Kanpur in the year 1985. Soon our contact developed into close friendship and then into a family relationship, which grew stronger with time. Interacting with him on matters of common concerns and life cleared many of our doubts.

Though silent from outside, Shri Mittal has always been a deep thinker. The negativity of the society, at times, used to upset him and he would often share his agony with me. However, his discussion was never perceived negatively as he attributed this trend to the ignorance of mankind and improper teachings. His resolve was to remove this ignorance in a manner, which would create least disharmony. His own concepts of life were clear and I encouraged him to share them with others. This contemplation ultimately galvanized in the formation of the 'Kabir Peace Mission' at Kanpur in the year 1990. Beginning with five founding members, the mission has now grown to a life membership of over 2000 spread all across the state of UP, India and even abroad. Shri Mittal's devotion and missionary zeal made this possible.

In this contemplative mood, Shri Mittal started penning down his thoughts, which took the form of very useful books. He first came out with a book, which consisted of large number of positive thoughts on various aspects of life. This book was well-received which encouraged him to write more and soon he came out with a collection of lessons learnt by him from his life, as he trained his mind to always extract a positive message from each experience. Eventually, such experiences took the shape of two more books titled the *'Positive Mind Power'* and *'Positive Mind Therapy'*. Both these books became extremely popular and helped many to organise their lives better.

This process continued in years to come and Shri Mittal expressed himself in the form of several other books namely, *'Laws of Positive Living'*, *'Think Positive and Things Will Go Right'*, *'Power of Positive Management'*, *'Power of Positive Words'* and several other collections. He also wrote several books in Hindi displaying the same positive state of mind. It has always been very gratifying for me to encourage and inspire him, which he valued greatly.

The present book of Shri Mittal's is on the same lines but with a difference. In this book, he has identified very ordinary interactions of life and has drawn a deep message from them. This way this book is full of wisdom, which is otherwise not available at one place in any scripture or self-help book. Going through this book, I wonder why such observations do not occur to most of us. The simple language and honest narrative of the events makes this book even more effective.

Shri Rakesh Mittal is a very humble person and feels shy even to take the credit for his writings. He considers himself only as an instrument of expressing divine wisdom. Even in the face of tremendous personal distress, I have never found him sad, nervous or depressed. He takes life as it comes and tries to make best use of it. No wonder he is an inspiration to others and his writings are highly motivating. What is heartening is that he is able to inspire the youth, which is our biggest resource. He is able to communicate with them not only through his books but through his personal interactions also. The present book, I feel, will be able to achieve this objective even better.

I would like to mention few words for his wife Arunaji also. She has made great sacrifices and has devoted her full energy in looking after her husband and her two sons, Amit and Rohit. As a result, Shri Rakesh Mittal has been able to devote his full energy in taking forward the work of Kabir Peace Mission without distraction. I salute her for this contribution to the society.

With these words I bless Shri Rakesh Mittal and hope this book will prove highly beneficial to the society.

16/16 Civil LinesKanpur-208001　　**Krishna Behari Agarwal**
Phone: 0512-2305416, 93361-18750
President
Kabir Peace Mission

Contents

Foreword		*v*
Blessings		*vii*
01.	Stone for Brick	1
02.	Cobbler Saint	4
03.	Never too Late	6
04.	There Maybe God	8
05.	Most Spiritual Place	10
06.	New Year Call	12
07.	Loneliness or Solitude	15
08.	Children and the Core Values of Life	17
09.	Indiscriminate Renunciation	19
10.	Kaveri Water	21
11.	American Neighbour	23
12.	Many Houses, No Home	25
13.	Ancient Wisdom, Modern Times	27
14.	Divine Care	29
15.	Secret of Success	31
16.	How Many Miracles	33
17.	Marriage Technology	35
18.	No Fixed Deposits	37
19.	Without Appointment	39
20.	Success Has No Competition	41
21.	Ex-Father	· 44
22.	One Help Every Day	46
23.	Who is Not a Bahai	48
24.	Not Even a Nose Ring	50
25.	Half Dilemma Gone	52

26.	Magic of Pardon	54
27.	Power of Compassion	56
28.	Tiger's Dentist	58
29.	Oust My Son	60
30.	Investing in a Book	62
31.	What is Your Age	64
32.	Jealousy is Natural	66
33.	Cent Percent Negative	68
34.	Not by Default	70
35.	It is Quite Sufficient Sir	72
36.	Right on God	74
37.	Target vs. Goal	76
38.	How Poor We Are	78
39.	Cosmic Vision	80
40.	Crime vs. Sin	83
41.	Rich Man's Diwali	85
42.	Diversity in Unity	87
43.	Spiritual Journey	89
44.	Everything is All Right	91
45.	Wedding Lunch	93
46.	Backbone of India	95
47.	No Help is Small	97
48.	Sauce and Rice	99
49.	Catholic or Protestant	101
50.	Nam Sankirtan	103
51.	I Will Buy It	105
52.	Old Newspapers	107
53.	Breaking Steel Ingots	109
54.	Universal Consciousness	111
55.	Was It a Help	113
56.	One in Six Billion	115
57.	Blaming the Tools	117
58.	Grace of God	119
59.	For Our Sake Only	121

60.	Forty Out of Forty	123
61.	Trials and Triumphs	125
62.	Aloo Bukhara (Plum)	127
63.	Talk to Strangers	129
64.	Let God Decide	131
65.	What is the Difference	133
66.	Hen with Golden Egg	135
67.	One Step At a Time	137
68.	The Nail Came Out	139
69.	Second Class Yogi	141
70.	Land for Grave	143
71.	Metamorphosis	145
72.	Artificial Gold	147
73.	Malaysian Driver	149
74.	Pet on the Road	151
75.	NCC Camp	153
76.	Anil Ambani's Lunch	155
77.	Inner Management	157
78.	Both Disappointed	159
79.	Refusal by Coolie	161
80.	The Coffee Machine	163
81.	Secret of Economic Growth	165
82.	No Change in Medicine	167
83.	Honour of the Back Seat	169
84.	Joy of Ignorance	171
85.	Went Without Dinner	173
86.	A Stitch in Time	175
87.	People Honour the Honour	177
88.	How Much Do We Need	179
89.	Do it with Calm	181
90.	Breakfast is the Same	183
91.	When We Think Positive	185

Stone for Brick

I had a friend who lived in Agra for a long time. I came in contact with him through another close friend at Lucknow. Soon our friendship turned into a family relationship and he became like my elder brother. At that time I was posted at Kanpur and had to travel quite frequently. Whenever an occasion arose I visited him at Agra, sometimes with family also, and enjoyed his hospitality. He was very popular in Agra and was well-known in the higher society.

In the year 1991, I shifted to Delhi on a central deputation. During my stay in Delhi, my friend's son got married and the ceremony was held in Delhi. The same was performed with lot of enthusiasm and dignity at a five star hotel located just opposite my residence. I along with my family attended the same and enjoyed the whole function. The son who got married was my friend's only son and was working jointly with him. After the marriage, they returned to Agra and the matter ended there. But we were still in contact.

In 1994, I shifted to Kolkata from Delhi on promotion, but used to travel to Delhi very often. It was at that time that I learnt through our common friend that my friend from Agra had shifted to Delhi with his wife. The tone of the message also did not sound very positive. He had also given me my friend's telephone number. So when I came to Delhi next, the first thing I did was to ring him up. I was keen to meet him and so was he. He was available on the phone and we fixed up a meeting at my guest house the same evening.

When we met, at the outset I asked him about the cause of shifting to Delhi and I also told him not to lie, if he really considered me a good friend. He was left with no option and told me the reality. The problem was the trouble created at home soon after his son's marriage. There was a serious problem of adjustment with the daughter-in-law, as a result to which separation became necessary. Since my friend had a small flat in Delhi and also some business interest, he decided to shift to Delhi along with his wife, but he was not happy about it. In addition to this, there were some problems with his brother also. All this had made him bitter and he was not taking all these developments very kindly. He ended by narrating his story that he would take the revenge of brick by stone.

Though I was quite concerned about his problems, I was not happy with his state of mind. I felt, that with such a state of mind, he was throwing the stones on himself while others had thrown only the bricks. But, he was not prepared to listen and asked me to keep my counsel to myself. Even then, I tried to pacify him and also gave some write-ups that were recently written by me. One of them was a write-up on JRD Tata under the caption 'When You Miss Your Wish'. In this write-up, it was derived that if sometimes providence does not fulfil our genuine wish, one should outgrow it and then we get much more than our wish would have given us. JRD Tata had no son but he gave all his employees the affection of a father. In the process, the Tata Empire not only grew, but grew magnificently. And he named his holding company as 'Tata-Sons'.

My friend perhaps, did not read the papers immediately because he was very angry with the treatment he received from his near and dear ones. But when he read this write-up after sometime, it worked. I remember to have received his call, late in the evening at Kolkata, when he told me that his family too would expand thereafter. He would consider all those coming in his contact as his children and derive joy out of it. By this time, he had also become somewhat cool towards those who had hurt him. I was very happy at this development. Thereafter, his compassion grew constantly and he became compassionate towards his son, daughter-in-law and brother also. Once this happened, all family relations became normal and they started visiting each other with even greater concern. Wittingly, I then told him that it was now that he had replied to the attack of brick by stone.

*****

Cobbler Saint

India is a country of saints and they come from all sections of the society – the rich, the poor, the low caste and the high caste. In fact, a true saint is above all these man-made divisions and essentially sainthood is a state of mind. There may, quite often be a confusion between what appears outside and what is inside. Between the two, the inner reality is more important and to be more true, the sole measure of sainthood. Unfortunately, in present times the emphasis is more on the external and therefore, true saints rarely come to light. We have a large number of persons who can be placed in the category of saints though they are never recognised that way.

I came across such a saint in Delhi in the year 1992. I was living there in a multistorey government colony located in R K Puram. Once, a strip of my bathroom *chappals* broke and I decided to get it repaired instead of replacing it. I thought that repair would cost me a maximum of five rupees, while the replacement could cost me much more. So I went to a cobbler who used to sit in a corner of the colony at a crossing. I always saw him doing his work with a lot of concentration and dedication. This attitude of his impressed me a lot.

When I went to him with my broken *chappal*, I found him in the same mood. When I requested him to repair the *chappals*, he did so promptly and gave it back to me. In a place like Delhi, even a small repair could cost as much as rupees five at that time. But I gave him a two rupee coin hoping that it would satisfy him. And I was greatly surprised when even without looking at me; he took out a one rupee coin from his collection and passed it to me. I silently took the coin and came back home with the repaired *chappals*. I felt, perhaps it was against his dignity to press for the acceptance of the whole amount.

The face of the cobbler is still in my mind and whenever I think of him, I pay him a silent tribute. To me he was a saint of the highest category. I am of the view that there are a large number of such saints in our country. That is why our nation is able to face all the challenges without any major turmoil. If at all any disturbance is created, it is by those who try to appear as saintly, but in reality are not. Let this message go to such persons.

*****

Never too Late

In the year 1995, I attended my graduation silver jubilee at the University of Roorkee in the month of November. It was a very healthy tradition of the University (now IIT) and it continues till date. Along with the silver jubilee, there is a tradition of celebrating golden, diamond and the platinum jubilees also. It is a moment of great joy and fun, in addition to the introspection when all the batch mates meet.

The same was the atmosphere during the celebrations of the silver jubilee meet also. There I met my first year room-partner also who used to be a very smart and intelligent boy. He came from a middle class family and became my room-partner in a double-seated room. Soon I noticed that he was falling into wrong habits like smoking, which subsequently graduated to drinking. He used to look very handsome while smoking and this fact used to encourage him further for the indulgence. Initially, when pointed out not to indulge so much, he used to listen, though he never followed the advice. Soon, he started raising objections against the counsel of good friends and gradually everyone stopped advising him.

As a result, he became a chain-smoker, started watching movies more frequently and also started missing classes. I don't remember if he could ever reach the mess for breakfast thereafter and at times, missed lunch too. For the remaining university days, his habits remained more or less the same, though being intelligent he could clear his examination and passed out with all of us. After great difficulty, he found a job.

Thereafter, we met only occasionally but his career graph was not going very well. His habits also started showing up on his health and he contracted several diseases, which are dangerous for human life. It was in this condition when he attended the silver jubilee meet. It was painful to see him in such a condition.

Fortunately, he had developed a feeling of guilt and confession by this time and met me in person to tell all of this. He almost shed tears when he said that he should have paid heed to my and other friends' advice right in the beginning. By not doing so, he paid a heavy price in terms of the quality of his life but it was too late. He also showed a firm resolve to undo all that had been done.

This made me very happy. I assumed that his resolve would take care of half his problems and the rest would fade with time, at least substantially if not fully. Fortunately, it went exactly the same way and today, he is doing well. For me also, it is a matter of great relief because somewhere, I also felt guilty as being his room-partner in the initial days, I couldn't help him. Truly, it is never too late to make a resolve in life.

*****

There Maybe God

In the year 1995, I had a chance of visiting China. At that time, I was posted as the development commissioner for iron and steel and the visit was in connection with the study of the steel sector in China. We were a group of seven persons led by me. It was a very useful trip and it gave us an insight of China's progress, their way of working and their future. There was a lot to learn from them notwithstanding the fact that all is not well with them also. People there did not appear free and could not express their opinion freely. Even personal beliefs of the people were greatly influenced by the government. That is why doubts are raised about its official progress vis-à-vis real progress. Anyway, this is just by way of giving a feel of the environment there.

In this visit, I had a very interesting experience. As usual, I was carrying few books for reading during this ten-day trip. One of them was *'Power of God'* and was published almost a century back. This book had been given to me by a friend on loan and I had to return it back soon. Therefore, I used to carry this book to read while I travelled. In China, we had the company of a younger interpreter who used to help us in our conversation. He was a handsome and smart boy, still unmarried. Within no time, he became friendly to us and we could talk on many subjects beyond our official matters.

When this young boy saw a book on God in my hands, he became curious and asked why I was reading such a book when there was no God. Chinese, in general, have been brought up in an environment that they don't believe in God. Though I knew about it, such a staunch denial for God came as a surprise to me. More than that, such a statement was a pointer to many limitations of the Chinese society. Then and there I threw a challenge to him that during my stay in China, I would make him believe in God.

Since he was in our company almost all the time, we had several occasions of discussion on various dimensions of human life and Nature. In these discussions, quite often, we used to reach a dead end, going beyond which was not possible without the assumption of a superpower, at which point; he had a tendency to escape. But certainly, he used to feel trapped though he didn't want to accept the existence of such a power because of his strong beliefs and also because of the prevailing socio-political environment in China. Such situations arose several times.

When the visit was coming to end, I wanted to know the result of my efforts. When asked, he honestly admitted that "There Maybe God." This was far beyond his initial statement that "There is no God." For me, it was a partial victory.

*****

Most Spiritual Place

In July 1999, I got a chance of visiting Malaysia and Singapore along with my wife. There was a conference on 'security management' at Penang in Malaysia in which I was invited to address a lecture on 'Security – An Inner State of Mind' and it went well. On our way back, we stayed at Singapore for four days. It was during these days that I was invited by Singapore Jaycees to speak on the subject 'how to be positive and motivated at all times' and I was looking forward to the same. The convener of the programme was a young member of the club and he was to pick me up from my hotel.

According to me, being positive and motivated at all times is what contributes to becoming a highly spiritual person. So, I was planning to speak on those lines. I was also carrying a book authored by me, titled *Spiritual Lessons from Life*. This book was in my hands when the convener was taking me and my wife from the hotel to the venue of the talk. Seeing the title of the book, he became somewhat skeptic about the success of the programme. He advised me not to speak on spirituality, as this word was not familiar in Singapore and there were good chances of the programme turning into a disaster. I was amazed, though I kept silent. But inside me, I decided to speak only on spirituality and nothing else. In a way, it was a challenge to my concept of spirituality, which I got from my spiritual master.

After the initial formalities were over and as I stood to speak, my words were "Dear young friends of Singapore, it is a great pleasure to be in Singapore for me and my wife. I have not seen a more spiritual place than this in my life. There is excellence, orderliness, sense of purpose, efficiency, courtesy, concern, cleanliness, sincerity and other good qualities, all around. According to me, spirituality is nothing but a combination of these qualities. The only difference is that you are not aware of these great qualities of your own." These opening remarks were received with great applause and thereafter, communicating with them became very easy. Our interaction continued for almost three hours against the stipulated time of two hours. After the talk, all copies of the book titled *'Spiritual Lessons from Life'* were bought by the participants and it was now the turn for the convener to get amazed. However, it was not his fault. The word 'spirituality' has always been interpreted very narrowly. In reality, it is the infinite expansion of the mind and once such a state is achieved, we always remain positive and motivated.

*****

New Year Call

India is a big country and it is a great country too, but not all of us understand its greatness. Most of us only look into its shortcomings and address them without suggesting a solution and much less doing something in that direction. The reason is that we don't try to understand India and instead keep on judging it. It is often said that there is unity in India's diversity and sometimes the same is said in a reverse manner. Whatever be the manner of saying so, it is a fact. I had a first-hand experience of this in the year 1999 in Tamil Nadu, where I had gone as an election observer in the Parliamentary election.

My place of duty was Ariyalur in Perambulur district. Now it has been made an independent district. At Ariyalur, my stay arrangement was made in a government cement factory where I reached late in the evening. I was to stay there for about three weeks, though with gaps. The place was comfortable and there appeared to be no major problem except the monotony of south Indian food. The constituency was considered to be a peaceful one.

After a good night's sleep, as I was preparing to come out of the guest house for a morning walk, I noticed a short elderly person wearing half-pant and a rule in hand waiting in the lounge. As I was coming out of my room the gentleman intercepted me with a question. He wanted to know whether any observer was there from Lucknow and if yes, who that was. He must have come to know about it from the guest house authorities or the local revenue officials. When I told him that it was me, he felt very happy and gave me an offer. He said that his name was Perumal and he had remained posted at Lucknow for a long time in the Army Medical Corps and was settled in Ariyalur after retirement. He further said that being a north Indian, I might face problems with the food, as *chapatis* were not available in the guest house. Since his wife knew how to make *chapatis*, he offered me *chapatis* whenever I wished to eat them. I could tell the caretaker and he would arrange the same from his home.

I was deeply touched by the offer. I immediately realised that he was a very good person and gratefully accepted his offer without any serious intention of invoking the right he had given to me. Then I enquired more about him. His house was very near to the guest house on the main road. I also accepted his invitation to visit his home. More than anything else, his offer made me feel at home in that remote corner of Tamil Nadu, far away from my hometown. Subsequently, I learnt from officials at the guest house, as well as the revenue department that he was a very popular person in town and was very helpful too.

After becoming sure of his credentials, one morning during my walk I felt like visiting his house, which was very near. He had a very simple house with natural surroundings. All his children were well-settled and he had great pride in talking about them and also in saying how he and his wife had made sacrifices in order to bring them up. Most of the time they lived separately for the sake of their education and it was only in Lucknow that they stayed together for a couple of years. That was how she had acquired *chapati* making skills. I enjoyed spending some time with him over a cup of coffee.

Thus, our affection grew during my stay at Ariyalur and I visited him one or two more times. Once I invoked my right of getting *chapatis* from his home, more to show respect to his kindness than out of real need. He joyfully obliged, though it was a different matter that according to north Indian standards the stuff was anything but *chapatis*. But the affection of his family was very much evident in the product. The affection continued to grow thereafter, as he kept in touch with me over the telephone and through letters after the election. And I was amazed with joy when the first New Year call in the year 2000 was from Mr Perumal. Till today, the first call I receive on every New Year is from Mr Perumal at 5:30 a.m. sharp. Isn't India great?

*****

Loneliness or Solitude

Human Life in general is a long journey. Each life is an exclusive one and takes its own path. Perhaps no two lives have ever followed the same path or will ever do. However, two facts of life are the same i.e., birth and death. On both these occasions, one is alone. Whether we like it or not, no one can escape death and also no one can give us company at the time of death. If this fact is well accepted by us, the fabric of life changes for the better and we live in this world with great peace and harmony. In this achievement our riches, positions or fame hardly play any role.

This realisation came to me even more clearly, after reading the autobiography of Justice M C Chagla, an eminent personality of India, titled *'Roses in December'*. Chagla's life was a constant success story, always on the ascent from worldly point of view. He rose from one position to another without ever looking back and occupied many high positions most of us wish for. In a way, his life must have been envied by many of his contemporary colleagues. But after reading the book I realised that no life is to be envied because no one knows others internal agonies.

After a long, active and successful career, Dr Chagla also had his lonely days. His wife had passed away before him and children had settled down away from him. So, in his last days he was physically alone. He was not prepared for such a life and he candidly admits this in his book. He always believed in a life of fun and not only that he looked upon those who didn't with a sense of awe. That is why at the end of his book he appended a small chapter titled, 'Personal' – an extract of which goes like this:

We have to distinguish between solitude and loneliness. Solitude is self-imposed, loneliness is thrust upon you. In solitude, you commune with yourself. You meditate and for the time being cut yourself off from the world. In loneliness, you are at war with yourself, realising the futility of life and the absurdity of existence, or the inability to resolve the conflict between the real and the ideal, between what is and what ought to be, between the temporal and the spiritual. I, therefore, have always loved company – to be alone is to me the worst kind of punishment that could ever be awarded for whatever sins I might have committed. Throughout my life I have had the company of someone or other, if of no one else, always of my wife. I have had my bitter moods and moments of unhappiness, but her death made me permanently unhappy, for I could never be sure of someone being by my side when I needed company most."

I find a great message in this paragraph. The fact is that we all are alone in this world. The so called company, which we look for and generally rejoice, is a myth. It is only an opportunity to learn the lessons of life in order to reach its goal. If one fails to understand this mystery, life is a waste irrespective of its external success. On the other hand, if this mystery is understood, one is never alone irrespective of the external conditions. Eventually, we have to be in our own company and we call that condition 'Solitude'.

'Loneliness' and 'Solitude' are two names given to the same condition with different frame of mind. No one can negate the fact of being alone ultimately. If we understand the mystery of life, we live in solitude and in the absence of this understanding, loneliness prevails.

*****

Children and the Core Values of Life

Once I was invited by a famous public school of Rampur to speak to children on the core values of life. This is a subject dear to my heart and so I accepted the invitation and a programme was fixed accordingly. As I reached the school and spent few minutes in the principal's office, I was cautioned by him that it was a difficult assignment for me, as children these days hardly understood the meaning of values. I was surprised to hear such a statement coming from a principal of a reputed school but took the advice in right perspective. It, however, had the effect of making me more determined to make my talk effective and I set my mind accordingly.

Soon, thereafter, I had to face a large number of students aged perhaps from 10 to 16 years. They looked enthusiastic and keen to listen. This encouraged me further and as I faced them my initial words were, "My dear young friends, your principal has asked me to speak to you on the core values of life, but I will not speak on them and in turn make you speak on values, as you are the true epitome of values and not us." This opening remark cheered them up and they prepared themselves for the ensuing interaction.

My next query to them was about the student who scored highest marks in class ten. There was a boy who stood and told me that he had scored highest marks in class ten. I asked him to come forward and tell others about the secret of his success. He told his fellow students that he worked hard and studied regularly and that was the secret of his success. At this, I posed a question whether 'working hard' or 'being regular in studies' were values or not. To this there was a collective response from the children that it was so.

Then I put another question and wanted to know if there was any one who liked to have a liar as a friend. There was none on which I asked whether they liked a truthful friend or not. To this there was a uniform response in the affirmative. Once again I asked whether 'truthfulness' was a value of life or not and there was no dissent on this also. In this way, I asked similar questions on other values of life like kindness, compassion, pardon, sharing, helping, etc., and not a single student had dissenting views on the fact that they all are core values of life, which are necessary for our happiness or success.

Having established my point, I told them why faith in core values of life was shaking these days, as was the intention of the principal and what we all needed to do to restore them. This was also done in a logical and convincing manner. I was pleasantly surprised by the positive response of children, which only reaffirmed my faith that children are the real epitome of values. The fault if any lies with us who fail to display these values in our lives and blame children that they don't understand values. My message was well-delivered during this interaction, which of course the principal also very graciously acknowledged.

*****

Indiscriminate Renunciation

Today, a very common misconception about being religious or spiritual is that such a person has to give up his or her worldly duties and has to lead a life of deprivation. Perhaps, such misconception has always been there but it is more so in the present when science has made us more rational and we want a logical explanation of any religious or spiritual message. As a result, most of those who have been imparted modern education keep themselves away from religion or spirituality. The very mention of these words draws before them a sketch of a person in saffron clothes doing nothing with this world.

Since my childhood I also carried this impression and kept myself away from any religious rituals. Moreover, I had noticed many so-called religious persons indulging in irreligious activities, which always created a doubt in my mind about the correct definition of religion. However, a time came in my life when I developed a keen desire to know the correct definition of religion and more than that why should one be religious in a true sense. Since the desire was keen and honest, I got ample opportunity to interact with the right persons, right organisations and right books. All this removed my doubts and I arrived at a conclusion that there is no conflict between being religious and being a successful worldly person. In fact, I feel they reinforce each other and give us the best of life. When we understand religion in this perspective, it becomes spirituality and all our misconceptions about religion or spirituality drop very naturally.

To establish this point, I would like to mention a portion of a book, which I read many years back. The title of the book is *'Play of Consciousness'* written by Swami Muktananda. In this book, *Swamiji* has described the journey of his spiritual life and in the process gives many pearls of wisdom. At one place, he gives a very interesting definition of 'bondage' and 'freedom'. When asked about the difference between the two, he says that 'indiscriminate renunciation' is bondage, while 'discriminate indulgence' is freedom. It means that in order to achieve freedom one has to be a wise person.

Those who think that freedom is achieved only through renunciation or indulgence are always led towards bondage and are wrong. The secret of freedom lies in between. When we renunciate indiscriminately, in all probability it leads to bondage instead of liberation. Thus, all of us are expected to perform our worldly duties sincerely but detachedly in order to get freedom. Such type of indulgence is discriminate indulgence and leads to happiness or freedom. If we understand this fact correctly, we enjoy both the worlds – the secular as well as the spiritual.

*****

Kaveri Water

We as north Indians often learn of the Kaveri water dispute between Tamil Nadu and Karnataka, two most important southern states of India. Quite often, one also wonders why issues like this can not be settled amicably and what is so great about sharing river water. We also tend to blame politicians for not solving such problems. While this may be true to some extent, such matters are not so simple because behind such issues lie the genuine needs and sentiments of people. I realised this truth during my visit to Tamil Nadu in the year 1999 as election observer for the parliamentary election. The incident goes like this:

During the course of this duty, I also had the opportunity of visiting Madurai, the place famous for the Meenakshi Temple. While returning from there to the place of duty, the car passed through an area, which was the best in paddy cultivation and called the rice bowl of Tamil Nadu. My escorting officer told me that it was the Kaveri basin area and that the success of crops was mainly dependent on irrigation from the Kaveri water. The area looked so beautiful that I asked the driver to stop for sometime in order to watch the fields and enjoy the beauty of the lush green paddy crop. I had not seen such a beautiful paddy-field ever before and so, I spent almost half an hour in the fields.

As we started travelling again, soon we crossed the Kaveri River, which is split into four or five streams in that area. While doing so, the issue of the Kaveri water dispute came to my mind and all my previous perception about it disappeared. I could easily feel the need and sentiments of the farmers who are the beneficiaries of the Kaveri water. Perhaps, the same need and sentiments exist in Karnataka also. The accompanying officer told me that the whole livelihood of this area depended on paddy and if the crop fails, people face tremendous problems. I was silently agreeing with him.

The point being made here is not that the dispute should not be sorted out amicably. That it should be done is very necessary but the complication of such issues should be appreciated against the background of people's needs and sentiments. The joy of a lush green crop, to me, is invaluable and the mere site of it was enough to give me the kind of happiness, which no amount of money can buy. Therefore, in order to expand our personality, it is necessary to understand the feelings of people also, without always judging them and looking at the issues only from the point of view of economics or politics.

*****

American Neighbour

In the year 2000, I along with my wife had gone to attend the 'World Peace Summit' organised at the UN headquarters in New York, in the month of August. After the summit was over, we were staying with our nephew who was newly married and was living near New York. During the same period, Bhartiya Vidya Bhavan had organised a programme under the caption 'Vande Matram' in which the then Prime Minister of India, Shri Atal Behari Vajpayee was the chief guest. Being a life member of Bhartiya Vidya Bhavan, I was also invited in the programme and I had arranged an additional invitation for my nephew and his wife. My nephew was living in a small flat on the first floor and there was another similar flat opposite to his on the same floor. There was a common entrance for both at the ground floor and my nephew and his neighbour both possessed separate keys of that entrance gate. Except for this, they did not communicate with each other, as it turned out following the event given below.

We had gone to Bhartiya Vidya Bhavan's programme after breakfast and while returning in the afternoon, my nephew noticed that he had lost the keys to his flat including that of the common entrance gate. By the time he realised this we had almost reached home. He also realised that he had forgotten to pick up his bunch of keys after it was passed through the screening machine at Bhartiya Vidya Bhavan for security reasons. We had already travelled a lot and there appeared no sense in going back to the venue of the programme. So we decided to deal with the situation accordingly.

When we reached home, we thought of taking the neighbour's help in getting the common entrance gate opened. But my nephew didn't have his telephone number. Somehow, he managed to get in touch with him through the locality office and requested him to open the common gate. During all this activity, me and my wife were silent spectators, hoping that the neighbour would at least offer his flat for waiting and also offer a cup of tea or a drink, which we needed badly. However, when the neighbour came down to open the common lock, he was accompanied by a big dog and after opening the lock, rushed back in a very impersonal manner. All our hopes for comfortable waiting and a drink were shattered in no time.

Anyway, we kept waiting and sat on the stairs while my nephew was arranging for a locksmith who came in about half an hour. After opening the lock of his flat in almost no time he charged fifty dollars as his wage. During this entire wait, we were fondly remembering our country where most of us consider it our good luck to help our neighbours, particularly in time of crisis. But in America, hoping for such courtesies was perhaps our ignorance. It also occurred to me that we should not follow the West blindly, so that our human qualities disappear. After all, India is a country which has always believed in the concept of 'Vasudhaiva Kutumbkam', the entire world is our family. It is a different matter that even the nuclear families are now breaking up in increasing numbers.

*****

Many Houses, No Home

I worked as a housing commissioner of UP for more than two years. It was a period of great achievement and satisfaction. Many new schemes and projects were initiated or brought to logical end during this period. The greatest satisfaction and joy was experienced when those who had no hope for shelter could get a dwelling unit in the normal course, without any bribe or push. Even a small unit of house gave the homeless so much joy that quite often tears used to roll down their eyes when the allotment letter was given to them. Many such scenes still appear before my eyes when I think of them. I still keep encountering many such beneficiaries who feel so obliged because of such valid allotments and tell me how they are enjoying their small homes.

On the other hand, there used to be equally large number of applicants who did not need a house or plot for their immediate use. Their sole purpose was either speculation or just future apprehension. This was the group, which also applied pressures through various sources or even offered bribe openly. While I tried to deal with all such cases on merit, I was not always successful. At times, property had to be allotted to such persons at the cost of more needy applicants. But as an individual, I couldn't do much as such allotments were not illegal in the strict sense of the term. Certainly, they violated the principle of equity or social justice.

One day, an applicant falling in the above category came to see me in connection with a plot allotment. He appeared to be charming in his manners so I started talking to him at a personal level. During the course of our talk, I discovered that he already had four residential properties in various towns and had applied for the fifth one. Also, either he had no family or had separated from his family. In a way, he was a loner. Still, I thought of considering his case or merit. In the same connection I also asked for his address and where he actually lived. At this, he was a little perplexed and could not respond immediately. Perhaps he was apprehending some enquiry by the housing board. So he frankly said that though he had given an address on the application form, the fact was that he had no home. Therefore, if any enquiry were to be conducted, in all probability he would not be available on the given address.

A majority of such applicants who were rich or occupied an influential position with a dwelling unit of their own did not necessarily use the houses allotted to them. They were also confused about the place of their settlement. Moreover, matters like in whose name the property should stand, mode of payment, time of possession, etc., also added to their confusion. It was also very difficult to convince them that they didn't need the property.

While his ambiguity about sharing his home address was sufficient reason to reject his application, it was amusing for me to see a person with many houses and no home.

*****

Ancient Wisdom, Modern Times

*T*wentieth century saw mind-boggling progress in the field of science and technology, particularly in the later half of this century. It is said that the progress made in this period surpasses the achievement in the field during many millenniums. However, the cost of this achievement has been very high in the sense that for this progress we lost the wealth of our ancient wisdom. No wonder that despite all the materialistic progress, human happiness has come down drastically and the society is facing a period of conflict, confusion and chaos. We need to contemplate on this issue seriously so that the human race achieves not only progress but peace also.

The whole world started realising this situation towards the end of twentieth century and many positive forces came forward to work in this direction. I got the opportunity to participate in two such initiatives during the year 2000 itself. The first occasion was the address of the world's spiritual leader, Dalai Lama from the precincts of Sarnath in Varanasi. This is the place where Gautam Buddha gave his first discourse after enlightenment. The event started with a '*Deep-Yagya*' on the bank of the Ganges in which several spiritual and social leaders of the country took part. Lighting of the Lamp is a symbol of removing ignorance and imparting knowledge. This symbolic ceremony was received well and in a way the twenty-first century began with a vow of lighting a lamp instead of cursing the darkness.

In the forenoon of 1ˢᵗ January 2000, Dalai Lama gave his message to the entire world. The central message of his address was that we must make use of ancient wisdom in order to make best use of the material progress on account of scientific development. Both are complimentary to each other instead of being in conflict. Our ancient wisdom lays emphasis on core values of life, which are necessary to follow if we want peace. May be some modifications in the interpretation of our scriptures are required, but their spirit has to be followed as such. If we do so, our conflicts and confusion will reduce greatly and disappear in due course.

The second event was the meet of the world's spiritual and religious leaders at the UN headquarters in New York. In this event, about 2000 delegates from almost all countries of the world participated and deliberated on the subject of 'peace'. It was noticed that human nature is essentially the same irrespective of place, language, colour, religion, caste and creed. All want peace and the mad race for material progress is also an effort to achieve the same objective. It is a different matter that in the absence of core values, we fail to find it. The central message of this meet was also the same that we need 'Ancient Wisdom' in order to make best use of 'Modern Times'. Let us all try to follow this in our lives in order to be successful, as well as peaceful.

*****

Divine Care

I got an opportunity of visiting South Africa in July 2001. At that time, I was holding charge of the horticulture and food processing department. Only few months before the visit I had read a book titled, '*Satyagrah in South Africa*' written by Mahatma Gandhi on his life in South Africa. In fact, his stay in South Africa had converted Mohan Das into a Mahatma. Over all, it is a very inspiring book and since then I was entertaining a wish of visiting South Africa. Providence provided this opportunity to me very soon and I was looking forward to this visit very keenly.

In South Africa, our main programme was in Johannesburg but we got an opportunity of visiting Durban also, which had been the main centre of activity of Gandhiji in South Africa. At Durban, the state agriculture minister was of Indian origin and he had hosted a lunch for our delegation. During this lunch I met the director of agriculture of the state who was also of Indian origin. Somehow we developed a liking for each other and he invited me for a cup of tea at his residence. Since I had some spare time and also wanted to eat some home made food, I readily agreed and he took me to his home in the afternoon. This home visit gave me a good insight of life in South Africa and the role of Indians in the progress of that nation.

During the course of our interaction, I asked my host to make available or suggest a book, which could give me an insight into the life of Indian migrants in the early days. On this request, he presented me a book on the life of a great social worker named Ram Bharos whose parents had come to South Africa towards the end of the nineteenth century. His parents died when Ram Bharos was not even 10 years old and also left to his care a younger brother with unsound mind. Both these boys found shelter in an orphanage after the death of their parents. Soon, the younger brother also passed away leaving Ram Bharos alone, to be brought up in the orphanage.

The young Ram Bharos turned out to be an intelligent and hard working boy who endeared himself to the management of the orphanage very soon. The manager in charge of the orphanage was himself a very good person and could notice the talent of Ram Bharos. So he gave him full support and encouraged him for higher education. Ram Bharos not only contributed his services in the running of the orphanage, but also paid attention to his education thereby passing the necessary examinations. So much so he was appointed in the orphanage itself on a responsible post. Further noticing the talent of Ram Bharos, the manager in charge also married his daughter to him and subsequently gave him the responsibilities of managing the orphanage. Ram Bharos not only carried out this responsibility very well but contributed in the field of social service so much, that his name and fame spread all over the country. In due course, he became a famous social worker not only in South Africa but in other countries also. The book on his life was written very objectively and I found it not only informative but touching also.

While I was going through the book in my hotel room, tears started rolling down my eyes. I became very emotional to notice that we all are under divine care but due to ignorance we feel that we care for ourselves. If an orphan boy in a country thousands of miles away from his native place could grow so well, where is the need of worrying for those who have no such uncertainty. My view is that we should do our best in our present and never worry for the future. Eventually, it is the divine power within ourselves, which takes care of us.

*****

Secret of Success

Today Mr E Sreedharan is a well-known personality not only in India but also in the world. The way he executed the Delhi Metro Rail project, is a matter of wonder in engineering as well as the management field. He is a simple man with deep spiritual roots and lives a value-based life. This is a great message to those who believe that in present times crookedness is necessary for success. I think that more important than this physical contribution to India, is his contribution to change the mindset of our people. I hereby narrate my first interaction with him.

This happened in November 2001 at Centre for Inner Resources Development (CIRD) in Vasundhara colony of Ghaziabad. CIRD is the name of my spiritual master's *ashram*, which was established just a year back. His name is Swami Bhoomananda Tirth and his main base is in Kerala at Trichur in the name of 'Narayana Tapovanam'. In November 2001, *Swamiji* had organised a two days programme for senior management executives on the subject 'beyond excellence'. I was one of the participants in this programme. There I found that Mr E Sreedharan was also a participant and that he too was *Swamiji's* disciple. Naturally, this gave me a sense of joy as well as elation, as I had great regards for him on account of his contribution to the Indian Railways.

At Lunch, on the first day itself, we happened to be together at the dining table. After a brief introduction of my background during the meet, I posed a question to Mr Sreedharan about the secret of his success and I also put a condition that I would be happy if the answer could be in one line. To this, his response was even more interesting. He asked why I wanted a one line answer as he could give the same in one word. This raised my curiosity even further, and I was keen to know that single word. Then very gently and with great sobriety he said, the secret behind every success is the 'integrity' of the leader and his people. This was enough for me and I needed no further explanation.

Now it was my turn to contemplate over this magical word called 'integrity'. All of us know this word and mostly give the certificate of integrity to our subordinates and expect the same from our superiors also. But are we really integrated in the true sense. I realised that 'integrity' is not a word; it is a textbook, which has to be read, understood and lived all through our life. A state of total integrity is perhaps our imagination, and we can only try to achieve it to the maximum extent. But if we do so, we have done our duty towards ourselves and the society.

This contemplation also took me to the *'Bhagwat Gita'* in which, the first three verses of chapter sixteen give twenty-six virtues of a perfect man. Normally, one feels that being honest only makes us perfect. But the reality is far away. One has to cultivate several good qualities in order to be successful in this world. If one doesn't, he has to face failure and in that situation, he attributes its causes to his existing good qualities instead of the missing good qualities. That is why the belief that crookedness is necessary for success prevails. The fact is that even those who have such beliefs are worried about the loss of values in the society.

I believe that this one word of Mr E Sreedharan needs lot of debate, discussion and clarification. Integrity is essential not only for mundane success but for spiritual success too. Any compromise with it is a self-defeating proposition and eventually all have to become victims of the same. The sooner we realise it, sooner shall we be able to achieve our true potential, both in the outer as well as the inner field. Truly, the secret of success everywhere is 'integrity'.

*****

How Many Miracles

There is a town near Delhi known as Mohan Nagar that is named after the family who established this town. The flag unit of this town is Mohan Meakins and its chairman is Col. Kapil Mohan. The life story of Col. Mohan is very inspiring. He is not only a good entrepreneur but also a good human being. Starting as a non-believer, he turned into a staunch devotee of Maa Durga and has constructed a very magnificent temple dedicated to her. In fact, my curiosity to meet Col. Mohan grew only after visiting the temple. Soon this opportunity also came and we spent sometime together. In the process, we developed a liking for each other.

After a year or so of this meeting, I had another opportunity to interact with him; this time in an informal manner. The CEO of Mohan Meakins, who happens to be a good friend of mine, had invited me for dinner. After the dinner he took me to Col. Mohan who was at his dinner table at that time. Col. Mohan called us at the dinner table and we started talking. I noticed that his food was very simple which is a reflection of his personality. While engaged in talking, Col. Mohan suddenly drew my attention towards the ring he was wearing in one of his fingers and said that the same was given to him by Sathya Sai Baba. He also said that the ring was collected by Baba from space. Further, he asked me if I believed in such miracles.

I had already heard of many such incidents but I hold no specific opinion about them mainly because such an opinion hardly matters to both believers as well as non-believers. So I responded accordingly and opined that we considered such events as miracles because we were not used to them. In my opinion, every event of Nature is a miracle but since we watch them happening every day throughout our life, we don't consider them so. I gave the example of digestion of food, which I was watching, as we were on the dinning table. Our role in this process is limited to gulping the food. The rest of the process is taken care of by nature without our notice or effort on our part. The large variety of fruits, plants and flowers we see around us is a miracle to me. Col. Mohan was convinced with this argument and our interaction shifted to other matters.

I contemplate over this issue quite often. The more I think in this regard, the more I notice the mystery of Nature. The best creation of Nature, a human being, is perhaps the biggest miracle and like this every creation of Nature is a miracle. Thus, how many miracles of Nature shall we count? We being equipped with the power of 'thinking' and 'intellect' start believing that we are the doers. This is nothing but ignorance because these powers have also been bestowed to us by Nature. Let us, therefore, live in tune with Nature and make best use of the many wonderful faculties provided to us.

*****

Marriage Technology

I had a friend who was a professor in mechanical engineering in IIT Kanpur, during the mid-eighties. During that period, I was also posted at Kanpur. Since he happened to be a relative of my wife and was a nice person by nature, we grew close and often visited each other. He had three daughters and one son who was the youngest in the family. All the children were bright in their studies and grew well. The son passed his engineering from BHU and did his masters as well as PhD from USA. Thereafter, he started working in USA but our contact continued. This boy, apart from being good in studies was also a good *tabla* player, photographer and artist. All these made his personality very pleasing.

This boy was married in the year 2000 in India, but I couldn't attend his marriage though I wanted to. In USA, he was working in Denver and is continuing to do so there. In 2002, I got an opportunity to visit Denver in connection with a 'book fair' where one of my books was to be released. This was to be in the month of June. In the month of March, I met him in Delhi and when I told him about this forthcoming event, he insisted that I must come and stay with him. His presence there thus became an additional attraction and I decided to participate. I was also keen to meet his wife, as I had not met her.

At Denver, he received me at the airport alone, though I was expecting his wife also. I had also very fondly carried a gift for her. But soon after we left the airport, my nephew told me that he had not shared a development with me. Then he told me that his marriage had failed and he was living alone in a studio flat. This was a kind of shock to me but I took it cool. I was in Denver for four days and during this period he shared a lot with me, which not only gave him lot of consolation but strength also to face the reality gracefully. However, one thing was sure that the event had changed the boy and he had become scared even with the word 'marriage'.

Throughout my stay at Denver and till today I often contemplate over this issue. While USA has developed all the possible technologies of the world and countless objects of comfort for mankind, surely no one will deny that it has failed to produce happiness out of all these. Take the example of marriage itself. A successful marriage contributes a great deal to happiness in life. While most of the marriages in lesser developed countries are successful and last for an entire life, this is not true in the case of developed countries. In a country like India, the institution of marriage is still very strong and is sustaining relationships well.

Surely when it comes to the technology of marriage, India beats most of the developed countries.

*****

No Fixed Deposits

There are a large number of organisations and institutions engaged in social activities. Most of these claim to be doing selfless service to society for a good cause. At the same time, we come across a good number of such bodies that collect money by various means including dubious ones with hardly any visible service. We also notice many of them closing their shops sooner or later. It, therefore, becomes a matter of consideration how to sustain a social organisation in order to achieve its objectives. One common way is to create enough fixed deposits and run the organisation out of the interest income.

Once I was contemplating over this matter in reference to Kabir Peace Mission. At that time, the organisation was in its childhood stage and the only source of income was its membership fee. For us too, one of the options was to create a corpus by seeking donations, but I was not very comfortable with this option. It was at this time that I came across a book of Mahatma Gandhi titled *'Satyagraha in South Africa'*. This book is a very good account of the Mahatma's days in South Africa. In fact, it was during this period that Mohan Das was converted into a Mahatma. Overall, it is a very touching narration of events.

Somewhere in this book Gandhiji had mentioned about the sustainability of his movement in South Africa. It was a great task and required a lot of resources particularly, money and people. He got both but he lays the condition for this arrangement of nature. Gandhiji clearly mentions that when one undertakes a social cause, only three conditions have to be fulfilled. The first condition is that the cause should be a felt need for the society and not the fancy or whim of one or few individuals. In other words, the cause should be owned by the society. The second condition is that the leadership or leaders behind the movement should be totally selfless and the third equally important condition is that the working of the organisation should be transparent, irrespective of the creditability of the leader or leaders. Gandhiji concludes by saying that if these conditions are fulfilled, no fixed deposit is required and the resources will be made available by nature perennially.

In these words of Gandhiji, I got the answer to my dilemma. The idea of fixed deposits was totally dropped and the whole concentration was shifted towards the cause, selflessness and the transparency. Thereafter, the mission grew in an exponential manner with support coming from many sources. Incidentally, we now have some fixed deposits also which is the only cause of worry.

*****

Without Appointment

With the growth of civilisation, several man-made laws, customs and practices have come into existence. Their main objective is to create order, convenience and efficiency in the society. They are also important for the protection of an individual's freedom, dignity and happiness. With the increase of pressure on the individual's time due to several modern developments, the need for them is increasing day by day. As a result, we are becoming lonelier and paying its price in a different way.

I had such an experience few years back in the USA. I was in Denver staying with a nephew of mine who was alone at that time. He used to take me for outings whenever it was possible to do so. He was a nature lover and the surroundings of Denver provide plenty of natural beauty. On one such outing, he mentioned that a brother of the Indian magician P C Sarkar lived nearby, in a beautiful house on the bank of a lake. He also told me that he was a frequent visitor to that house and was always welcome there. He further added that he would show me the house from a distance, as going inside without an appointment might be inconvenient to the family.

Being generally aware of the American way of living, I was in agreement with him. While returning from the outing, he took a detour in order to show me Mr Sarkar's house. Soon we arrived there and he stopped the car at a short distance from where Mr Sarkar's house was visible. It was a beautiful house and I had some desire to see it from the inside. Besides, after a long drive I was feeling the need for a cup of tea also. But I left it to my nephew only.

Incidentally, when our car stopped and we came out of it, Mrs Sarkar was outside the house watering her lawn. She immediately recognised my nephew, who then extended his greetings to her. Responding to that she invited us inside. On this, my nephew became formal and said that it could be inconvenient for her as prior appointment was not sought. In reply she said it was not inconvenient at all as she was free at that moment. My nephew again, tried to be formal on which I intervened and persuaded him to accept the invitation.

Thereafter, we spent about half an hour with Mrs Sarkar going around, inside and outside the house. This was a very meaningful interaction, which greatly enriched us with many facts about American life and Indians' contribution to its development. A hot cup of coffee was an additional gain, which was indicative of true Indian hospitality. I thought to myself that there has to be a limit to man-made laws, customs or practices and man should have the power to refuse them.

*****

Success Has No Competition

We are living in an era of competition. Day by day the competition for success is becoming so intense that the very joy of living is being lost. What is worse is that the pressure of competition has engulfed our young generation also and this has resulted into several disorders. The increasing number of suicides among young students is mainly on account of this pressure. This is a serious issue and needs to be addressed correctly.

I had a first-hand experience of this narrow definition of success, when I was addressing class XII students of Delhi Public School in Delhi, few years back. It was a biology section with boys and girls almost in equal number. When I asked them about the goal of their life, all said that they wanted to become doctors. They also agreed that it was not possible for all to succeed in the entrance examination but the very thought of not getting selected made them miserable. Perhaps they had cultivated a very narrow definition of success in their minds. In short, success for them only meant becoming a doctor.

Over this, I gave a real example of my nephew (sister's son) who also entertained the desire of becoming a doctor while he was studying. He tried for the entrance after class XII, but failed. Thereafter, he sought admission in BSc, a two-year course at that time. He again tried after completing the first year of BSc but failed in that attempt also. Quite disappointed, he completed his BSc and gave a third attempt for the medical entrance with quite a good hope for selection. But third time also he could not succeed. Everyone was disappointed and thought that this boy will see no success in life.

But all were wrong including the boy. Having completed his graduation, he was left with no option but to seek admission in MSc. He chose agricultural botany as his subject and sought admission in a prestigious institute of Delhi. Gradually, he was coming to terms and started taking interest in his post graduate studies. He did well and after completion got admission for research in Australia. Having obtained his PhD from there, he completed his post doctorate from USA. Today, he is one of the leading bio-scientists cum entrepreneur of the world in his field. His success is not only a matter of pride to him but to all his near and dears.

Hearing this example of success all the students started wondering. Perhaps they started rethinking about their definition of success. I also told them that this was just an example and there were countless of them. All this changed the environment of our discussion in a very positive way and they all participated in it with an open and happy mindset. Many of them told me over tea that they felt very relieved and the pressure of competing in the medical entrance had reduced to a great extent. Naturally, I also felt very happy and satisfied.

Perhaps all of us need to realise this aspect of success. Having born as human beings, we are the most precious creation of Nature. Nature has also not made any two human beings exactly similar. It means that each of us is an exclusive creation of Nature and there is a purpose behind our creation. Our effort should be to know that purpose and achieve it. For this, none of us needs to compete with others and if at all there is competition, it is with oneself only. This way our life should be a process of self-improvement. Once we do so, we get not only worldly success but achieve the goal of our life also.

Surely, there is no competition in success. No wonder the famous philosopher J Krishnamoorti used to hate the word 'competition' as for him this is a synonym for 'violence'.

*****

Ex-Father

We are quite used to terms like ex-president, ex-mp, ex-prime minister, etc., but terms like ex-father or ex-mother are very surprising for us. But in modern times these terms have also come in vogue and are often used in western societies. No wonder these terms may gradually become part of the Indian society also. I first came across this term in the year 2002 when I was in USA. On a flight from New York to Denver, I was travelling alone sitting on an aisle seat. On my right, on the middle and window seats were two young boys who appeared to be twin brothers. They were about 10 years old and were busy in their own conversation. There was no elderly person with them.

Though I had noticed their presence as soon as the plane took off, they drew my attention after about half an hour. Their conversation, though not very clear to me, made me curious to know about them. Therefore, I intervened in their conversation at an appropriate moment and enquired about them and about the purpose of their journey. Then they told me that they are twins and were going to meet their ex-father. Explaining further, they also told me that their mother had divorced their father to marry some other person and their father also did the same. It also came out in conversation with them that it was not their first divorce and both their father as well as their mother had done so several times. At that time, they were living with their mother and new father and were going to meet their real father whom they referred as ex-father.

This is how I came across this term and it set me thinking about the change in relationships in modern times, which I still do. While I have no intention of sitting in judgement over such developments, certainly I feel that the subtle joy of relationships in modern times has been lost to a great extent. That is why there is an increase in loss of peace, tension, hatred and jealousy. If we are not able to feel joy with natural relationships, how can we find it with other relationships? While our ancient culture has talked of 'Vasudhaiv – Kutumbkam', the world is one family; the modern culture is finding it difficult even to keep one family intact.

Surely, there is a need of taking a re-look at our relationships and devising means to make them meaningful in a real sense. We had done so long back and perhaps for doing so once again; we have to learn from our past without shunning modern development so that we live in a win-win situation.

*****

One Help Every Day

Though the Kabir Peace Mission was established in early 1990, it was almost on the ground for about a decade. One can also say that it was running on the tarmac before take-off. In fact, it now appears that it was really so as is evident from what followed.

In January 2000, I dedicated my first book to Kabir Peace Mission, which was a Hindi translation of two English books of mine. The title of the book was स्वस्थ चिन्तन के पथ पर (Swastha Chintan Ke Path Par) and the book was released by the then human resource development minister of India Dr Murli Manohar Joshi, in a well-attended function on 14th January at Lucknow. Dedicating the book to the mission meant that all proceeds of the book were to go to the mission. I have no hesitation in admitting that I thought several times before taking such a decision. But I reached a conclusion that in doing so, the overall gain was to be more than the pain. Subsequently, I dedicated all my books to the mission only.

With this clarity in mind, the mission got its receipt books printed and the first receipt was issued on 14th January 2000. At that time, I also wished and prayed that let Nature send at least one help to the mission, so that we could serve its cause with greater confidence and concentration. Perhaps God found us worthy of His blessings as since then, the average of help has been more than one every day. A large number of persons came in contact with the mission through various forums and programmes. This enriched the mission both ways, in terms of serving its purpose as well as harnessing resources.

In a book written by Gandhiji, I read that for the success of any social activity, the required ingredients are – right objective, selfless service and transparency in working. Our effort has always been to achieve these qualifications and our prayer to God is also to keep us on this path. It also proves that any sacrifice is not a matter of self-deprivation but of self-preservation. When we give, we get more, maybe in a different form.

*****

Who is Not a Bahai

*O*ur society is divided on various counts. These divisions are on the basis of geography, religions, castes, languages, food habits, occupations, etc. While it is a fact that no two creations of Nature are exactly similar, it is also a fact that essentially the whole creation is one. The ultimate goal of life is to realise this fact and that state is the ultimate in our spiritual journey. Once we understand and move in the direction of this understanding, the duality starts diminishing and our disharmony with the world starts lessening. Eventually, all our conflicts disappear and we live in a state of perfect joy.

I had an interesting experience of this process few years back in Lucknow. The head of CMS schools there, Sri Jagdish Gandhi is a follower of Bahai faith. This faith is very liberal in the sense that it talks of universal brotherhood and believes in no rituals. The faith appeals to all those rational persons who find this lacking in other religions. To me also, the concept of universal brotherhood has always appealed and I find myself very comfortable in the company of such persons who believe so. One day, Sri Gandhi invited me for breakfast with a senior fellow of Bahai faith from USA, who was on a visit to Lucknow. It was a pleasure for me to accept his invitation because it was a good opportunity for me to know more about the Bahai faith apart from respecting the invitation.

We were at the breakfast table for over an hour and during this period we were so engrossed in the discussion that taking breakfast became a secondary affair. I was in agreement with almost everything the American friend said and perhaps, he also appreciated my way of thinking. When we rose from the table, he warmly asked if I was also a Bahai. Certainly, I am not a Bahai in the strict sense of the term. But to say no at that point of time, didn't appear appropriate to me. Therefore, after a pause of few seconds, I answered in the form of a question only. And my question was, "Who is not a Bahai?" This answer pleased him a lot and obviously he could understand the deep connotation of this statement, which came from me spontaneously. Thereafter, we took leave of each other after exchanging greetings and never met again.

However, this meeting and more so the concluding part of it, keeps coming to my mind wherever I notice any conflict on account of various divisions in the society. I always think that there can never be a conflict between the essential nature of two persons and if it is so, it is on account of our ignorance. Therefore, the need is to remove this ignorance and all our pursuits, whether secular or spiritual should also be for removing this ignorance. Greater is the success in this direction; greater would be the harmony in society. And ultimately, it should be possible for us to feel that we all are Bahai's. Not only that, we should develop similar feelings for other faiths also. After all, being a true Bahai only means to be a good person, who cares for others more than for himself. By this definition of a Bahai, a good Hindu, a good Muslim, a good Christian, a good Sikh and so on, are all the same.

*****

Not Even a Nose Ring

Mr T S R Subramanian has been an IAS officer of the UP Cadre. Having risen to the post of chief secretary in the state government and cabinet secretary in the central government, he retired few years back. After retirement also he is useful to the society and is serving it in many ways. Sometime after the retirement, he wrote a book under the title *'Journeys Through Babudom and Netaland'*. This book is a kind of biography as well as a good analysis of ground realities in our country, particularly in respect of administration and politics. The book has been very well received and created a good debate among those who find mention in it. I read it soon after its release and enjoyed reading it. My one line comment on this book is that it is dig on the system with depth. While it does not provide answers to the malady of the system, it certainly provokes the system to think about the answers. This way it serves a great purpose. Subsequently, the book was published in Hindi also.

Leaving this aspect of the book here itself, I am mentioning an incident narrated in the book, which left a deep mark on me. It relates to the period when Mr Subramanian was posted at Geneva, on a UN assignment. In the same office, there was an elderly class-four employee named B Singh who hailed from eastern UP. He was in Geneva for quite sometime and was very popular among Indian officers posted there. The reason was his helpful nature along with the wisdom, he had acquired on account of this trait. His counsel to all officers, particularly those posted newly was well received and everyone looked for his help at one time or the other. He used to live there with his family.

It so happened that during the period of Mr Subramanian's posting there, the wife of this employee passed away and Mr Subramanian visited his residence to pay his condolence. It was early afternoon; his apartment was a bare one-room flat. A few other Indians were there to share his grief. Singh had just returned after the cremation of his wife. He was dry-eyed, drained of all emotions, and talking more to himself than to the visitors in his home.

He said, "She died last night. The nurse asked me to come back early this morning. She was being bathed and the nurse asked me to remove her nose ring before the cremation. *Saab*, I have never seen her without the nose ring ever since I had known her and married her when she was a ten-year-old. She wore it all the time, in bed, while bathing; it was a part of her. I could not bear the thought of separating her from the diamond nose ring. I told the nurse that I don't want it, let it go with her. The nurse said that the metallic item could not be taken into the cremation. *Saab*, I tried to remove the nose ring; but my hands were trembling and I could not unscrew it. Finally, the nurse removed it and gave it to me. You see *Saab*; she could not even take this small thing with her when she went. But, you see people who madly collect houses and money and property they can not take it up with them."

*****

Half Dilemma Gone

Today, the society in general is facing a great dilemma about the values of life. The environment around us seems to be so vitiated that a common belief that 'values don't work' has taken deep roots. This belief persists at all levels and the youth is no exception. But when youth becomes the victim of such a dilemma, it is a matter of serious concern. Their dilemma should be removed at the earliest and all those who are seriously concerned about the future of the society should make efforts in this direction. The fact is that if addressed correctly, it is not very difficult to do so. My personal experience and belief is that the youth responds better in any discussion on values than any other group. And in this fact lies the hope for the nation and perhaps the whole society.

I am narrating here one such experience I had about few years back. Once I was on a visit to an educational institution and it was the beginning of the session. The educational institution had courses in engineering, management and computer sciences. When I was in a conversation with the vice chancellor in this room, he suddenly asked me whether I would like to meet the first year students of engineering, as it was the beginning of their session. Since I had sometime with me, I accepted the offer and an interaction session was organised.

During the interaction, I chose to speak on the question of values only because I thought that it to be appropriate to the occasion. So after initial pleasantries, I straight away put a question to the group of young boys and girls whether they had a dilemma in regard to whether values work or not. To my surprise, all of them faced such a dilemma as was evident from the hands raised by them. Almost all of them raised their hands and there were many who raised both their hands, such was their dilemma. This put a great challenge to me as removing such a dilemma was not an easy task and more so with less time available to me for the interaction. Still, I resolved to do my best.

With this background, I started interacting with them. It was a participative interaction, which made my task bit easier. Having myself gone through such a dilemma and finding an answer in due course was my conviction and I was sure of passing this conviction onto them, if not fully but at least partially. I found the young students very responsive and my reasoning or logics in favour of living a value-based life was being received by most of them approvingly. Still, there were many genuine doubts, which I tried my best to remove. Our interaction went for about an hour and I was quite satisfied with it.

Having finished, I again put up the initial question whether they were still in dilemma about values. Now the response was quite different in the sense that less than half the students raised their hand and those who had raised both the hands initially now raised only one hand. To me it was an indication of the fact that at least half of their dilemma had gone. I think it was quite a good success for a debut effort. More than personal joy, it was hope that I got from the youth. Surely, there is need for more effort in this direction.

*****

Magic of Pardon

Our administrative system is infamous for large numberof laws, rules, orders, etc. and they are always increasing in number. The aim of all of them is to make the governance good, efficient, transparent and judicious. Also, there are provisions of disciplinary action against the employees for their lapses. Occasionally, they are punished also, though it is difficult to say whether punishment is really changing the system for the better or not. I narrate here an interesting experience during my posting as principal secretary of Secretariat Administration Department (SAD) at Lucknow.

SAD is also responsible for the upkeep of secretariat buildings. For this a Management Officer (MO) or an assistant management officer (AMO) is posted for each major building. At that time, one lady officer was posted as an AMO for an important building and she was considered to be quite efficient. I was in the habit of taking rounds of the secretariat and during one such round of that building I noticed certain shortcomings. As a result, I gave her some instructions and expected compliance by a certain date. I fixed up an inspection again on that day. She assured me that my instructions would be complied with by that time.

When I reached that place again on the appointed date and time, I found that neither the instructions were complied with nor was the officer present there. It was a great surprise to me. I also noticed that no one in her office was aware of my instructions. Naturally, it annoyed me and as soon as I came to my office, I gave instructions for disciplinary action against the AMO. The office promptly put up the file and proposed suspension or adverse entry to the officer concerned. By the time the file came to me, my anger had cooled down and instead of approving the proposed suspension, I ordered for seeking her explanation first. A letter was accordingly issued to the officer.

The file again came back to me after about a week. By this time, an explanation from the officer had been received as well processed. However, the office had drawn the same conclusion as it had done before, perhaps more to please me than on merits. However, when I read the explanation it appeared quite satisfactory to me. The officer had prayed for unconditioned apology and admitted that the lapse had been inadvertent. Somehow, my instruction given to her slipped her mind and she could not act on them. She had also mentioned that the question of disobeying could not even occur to her mind. Considering all this, I decided to pardon her and closed the matter there itself.

The news of this decision spread throughout the secretariat in no time. Perhaps the incident had come to the notice of many and they were curious to know about the outcome. Some might have been planning to protest also in case I had taken a punitive action. But then, many rang me up or met me personally to convey their appreciation and told me that it had a salutary effect on others also. The concerned officer, who had not dared to meet me after the incident, also met me with tears in her eyes and conveyed her gratitude. I was in fact, pleasantly surprised to see the magic of pardon. I also thought how nice it would be if rules also provided for a pardon clause, which is not the case as of now. As a result, my instructions had been effectively complied with on the next day.

*****

Power of Compassion

Many years back I read a book of Dalai Lama titled 'Power of Compassion'. After reading the book for the first time, I realised the real import of the word 'compassion' and also how powerful it is when practiced in true sense. I also had a practical experience of this fact few years later when I was posted as housing commissioner of Uttar Pradesh.

As housing commissioner, I used to meet the public every afternoon in order to listen to their grievances. At times, the number of visitors used to be quite large but I always attended to all. One day during this meet, a daily wage employee of the organisation met me with a medical report of Sanjay Gandhi Post Graduate Institute of Medical Sciences (SGPGI). Most of the visitors used to meet me for their house-related problems, so it was something I was not exactly prepared for. The person appeared to be very sick and his report required an emergency operation, which was to cost about one lakh rupees. As a daily wager, he was not entitled to reimbursement from the organisation. He had come to see me for seeking special dispensation, which was not within the rules. He also mentioned that without the operation he would surely die within a short period while after the operation the chances of his survival were about fifty percent.

This was a difficult situation for me particularly when other visitors were waiting in the queue. At that moment, human consideration became more important for me than rules. I, therefore, immediately rang up the Director of SGPGI, who happened to be a good friend of mine, to go ahead with the operation and also assured him of the payment. However, I was not clear about its source and thought about it only after meeting all the visitors. At that time, an idea came to me that half the money should be contributed by the employees and half by the organisation. When I placed this proposal before the association of the employees along with a cheque of my contribution, they all agreed to it and the money was arranged accordingly. The sick employee was soon operated in SGPGI and the operation was successful.

After about a month during my visitor's time, the same employee was again in the queue with a medical fitness report. In that state of fitness, it was not possible for me to recognise him on my own. It was only when he reminded me of the help extended to him; I pleasantly recalled the whole incident. Obviously it gave me great joy and satisfaction. At that moment, I also recalled the book of Dalai Lama and once again realised the 'power of compassion', which I consider beyond all rules and regulations.

*****

Tiger's Dentist

Nature has created a mind-boggling variety of flora and fauna on this earth. At times, one questions the purpose of all this creation but it is our ignorance. The fact is that every creation of Nature has a purpose and whenever any particular creation ceases to have a purpose, it ceases to exist. Perhaps, that is the reason why many ancient species are extinct today while many new ones are appearing. The closer we study the secrets of Nature; the greater is our appreciation for its beauty and perfect administration. Once we realise that, we ourselves are part of Nature and live in accordance with its laws, our life also becomes harmonious and we enjoy it fully.

I had a very interesting experience of such a design of Nature few years back. As commissioner of the Lucknow division, I had within my jurisdiction the Dudhwa National Park, which is primarily a tiger sanctuary. On my first visit to the park, I met a forest service officer who was an authority on the wild animals. He knew a lot about tigers also. After reaching Dudhwa in the evening, he gave us company in the rest house and we had a long discussion with him over the evening tea, as well as the dinner. There were many questions in my mind, which he answered to my full satisfaction. Naturally, all of us were enriched as a result of this interaction and were in a better position to watch the king of all animals, which eventually didn't appear before us.

During the course of our discussion, the forest officer told us the secret of a tiger's good health. He said that a tiger never eats more than necessary and leaves its prey as soon as his hunger is satiated. He also told us that the tiger goes to sleep for a while after eating. At that time, a question arose in my mind as to how a tiger cleans its teeth. After all, he eats raw meat and it must be sticking to his teeth. Unless the teeth are cleaned, there is every chance of the meat getting rotten and causing an infection in the mouth. When I asked this question, he felt very happy. Though I was not very serious about the question he gave a very serious reply to it.

He said that there is a dentist for each animal and that the tiger too, has a dentist; a bird. When the tiger goes to sleep after preying, it keeps his mouth open and a particular bird waits for this opportunity. The purpose of the bird is to feed itself with the leftover meat in the tiger's mouth. In the process of doing so, the bird cleans the teeth of the tiger. In this way, the bird plays the role of a perfect dentist for the tiger and the tiger pays the fee by providing food to the bird. This understanding between the tiger and the bird never goes wrong.

*****

Oust My Son

When I was commissioner of Lucknow, a retired civil servant came to meet me in my office. I didn't know him closely and had only heard his name but he felt close to me. He had a personal problem and wanted me to solve it with the help of my official position. The problem was his only son who was married and was living in the same house, on the first floor. The son had been brought up with lots of love and was married in due course. The daughter-in-law was also to their liking, at least in the initial years of marriage. The son was not very sound financially but his wife also being a working woman, they were somehow managing by themselves.

To begin with, the family was living together with a common kitchen but gradually the kitchen had to be separated and the son shifted to the first floor. The house was owned by the father. In due course, even living as neighbours became difficult and things reached to such a pass that the father wanted his son to vacate the house. The son was not doing so, mainly because of financial reasons and this had become a bone of contention between the father and the son. The father had come to me to get his house vacated.

I listened to his problem patiently without intervening, till he finished. As soon as he completed, I asked him whether he had come to me thinking of me as a commissioner or as a well-wisher. I also told him that as a commissioner, I was not in a position to help him because it was his personal problem, but I could certainly be of help as a person provided he desired so. Being a good person, he could understand my point and agreed to listen to my personal advice.

Then I told him that the problem was not with his son but with himself. His attachment, expectations as well as his ego were the main cause of the issue. I also told him that if at all separation from them was an answer to the problem; he should vacate the house instead of asking his son to do so. He was listening to me seriously, which encouraged me to advise further. I said that according to me, separation was not the answer to the problem and in all probability it would only aggravate it. The answer lied in shedding the ego and developing an attitude of detachment in their relationship. For this, he should start treating his son as his tenant whose help could be sought only in an emergency. For this, even if nominal rent was to be charged, there was no harm in doing that too. After all, even if his son vacated the house, he would search for a tenant.

The elderly gentleman took my advice seriously and without speaking much thanked me and left the place. His body language conveyed that he was going to follow my counsel and he actually did. He met me again after a few months and thanked me profusely for having given him a very pragmatic advice. At that time, his wife was also with him and she was very happy too. They both admitted that the major fault was at their end and once they took care of that the relationship improved. Now they were living happily with their son as neighbours just like a tenant. Since then whenever we meet, he never forgets to mention this episode.

*****

Investing in a Book

A lot is said about good books. Good books are our best friends and can bring a great change in life. I have personally realised this in my own life. Till the age of thirty, I was not fond of reading books other than the course books. But a time came in my life when I started reading good books and they have enlarged my vision immensely. Not only this, as a result of this expansion I myself started penning down my experiences and by now they have been published in the form of many books. Since these books are based on real-life experiences, they have been found to be useful and have reached thousands of readers. This in turn has given me great satisfaction and joy.

One of my books is titled '*Swastha Chintan Ke Path Par* (स्वस्थ चिन्तन के पथ पर) and its cover price is one hundred rupees. One day, I received a phone call from a stranger in Lucknow who introduced himself as a reader of this book and conveyed his appreciation for it. His appreciation naturally gave me a pleasure but this pleasure multiplied when he told me the reason of his appreciation. He said that he had decided to change the flooring of his house before reading the book which was to cost him about one lakh rupees. However, when he read a chapter in the book on 'simple living', he started liking his flooring because essentially, there was nothing wrong with that except that it had become obsolete. As far as utility was concerned, it was perhaps more. Thus an investment of one hundred rupees in the book saved his one lakh rupees.

For a moment I also felt that this single call had paid back all my efforts in writing the book. I could think of no better investment than this with such a high dividend. The same holds true with all our investments in good things whether physical, material, intellectual or spiritual. On the face of it, they may appear to be paying no dividend but their intangible benefit is so high that it surpasses all tangible benefits. Whether it is good health, good mind or positive thinking, all these make a great difference in our life. A good book is perhaps the best investment from this point of view.

*****

What is Your Age

$\mathcal{L}$ife is full of problems. While some of them are created by Nature for a purpose, most of them are our own creations and that too without any purpose. A wise person is one who does not create problems for himself and also seeks a purpose behind the problems created by Nature. However, it is easily said than done. Most of us keep on creating new problems in addition to the existing ones. Life is thus spent in this process and its true goal is missed. Not only this, these problems are a constant source of worries and disturb our peace of mind.

I feel there is need for changing our attitude towards the problems of life. Most of them are trivial and get sorted out in due course. It is a fact that ultimately all our problems get sorted out or become redundant and if we keep this fact in mind, they will not disturb us much. When we look back at our life, we realise that many problems, which appeared so big at that time, look so petty now that we even laugh at our folly in being so upset about them. This is true for most of us and if so, should we also not adopt the same attitude towards our present or future problems. I have a very interesting experience to narrate in this regard.

One morning, I was sitting in my office at home. One of my friends is a frequent visitor to my place and it is always a pleasure to receive him. He is a senior engineer in a Government organisation and is rated as a very good officer. Hardly ever did he bring any personal or official problem to my notice, what to say of being upset for them. But that morning, he appeared upset and sought my permission to put his problem before me. By his body language I was able to understand the kind of problem he was likely to share with me.

I knew that I had no solution to his problem and at the same time I was sure that he himself was capable of sorting it out. Therefore, refusing permission for placing the problem before me, I asked about his age. Though it appeared strange to him, he told me that he had crossed fifty-two few months back. Then I asked him whether any of his problems, till that age, still remain unresolved now. Being an intelligent and good person he could immediately understand my intention. With a smile on his face, his response was that even the problem, which he was going to share with me, got sorted out and he need not share it with me. This response pleased me a lot and I appreciated his wisdom. It is a different matter that then he narrated his problem also but along with the solution with which I fully agreed.

Therefore, whenever we face a problem, an easy way to sort it out is to think that all our past problems got sorted out in due course and so the present problem will also find a way. Our getting upset or frightened only delays the solution. The quicker way out is to keep cool and to trust our inner strength, which is provided by Nature or God.

*****

Jealousy is Natural

The five greatest enemies of ours are said to be desire, anger, greed, attachment and ego (काम, क्रोध, लोभ, मोहए वं अहंकार). All these give rise to jealousy, which is the root of all evils and a most difficult one to conquer. It is said that a jealous man poisons his own food and then eats it. It should, therefore, be gotten rid of at the earliest. But to do so is a great challenge. However, if we proceed bit by bit starting from its genesis, it becomes easier to win over this enemy of ours.

Once I was addressing the students of a public school in Noida. The occasion was the distribution of prizes to the winners in a quiz contest. There were about 500 young boys and girls who came from different family backgrounds. They were not only smart but also intelligent as well as responsive. My address to them centred round values and positive thinking. They were listening to me very attentively. During my address, I told them that when we have negative traits in us, we ourselves are the first and biggest victims of it. While this logic appeals to all, sustaining it all the time is a different task. Knowingly or unknowingly, we somehow get carried away by our lower nature and start nurturing the evil traits in us; be they anger, greed, desire or jealousy. The need therefore, is to be on the guard all the time and in due course our negative traits will fade away.

After my address there was an interaction session with the students. Many of them asked very searching questions which I tried to reply to the best of my capacity. One girl very innocently raised a question about jealousy and asked whether it was not natural to be jealous. She was right in the sense that almost all of us feel jealous whenever we see any of our colleagues going ahead of us, whether in riches or position or fame. Perhaps, no one can make a claim that he or she never felt jealous of others at one time or the other. While I appreciated her question, my answer was that if jealousy was natural, our suffering on account of it is also natural. Once we focus on this aspect of jealousy, our effort to get rid of it will be more. Thus, this negative trait of ours can be won over by this reverse process of contemplation. The girl was satisfied with this answer and so was I.

The same is true with all such inner enemies of ours like anger, attachment, desire, greed, ego, etc. When we allow them to prevail upon us we are the first victims of them. On the other hand, when we practice virtues like compassion, pardon, humility, patience, contentment, charity, etc., again, we are the first beneficiaries. Once we start looking at evils and virtues in this perspective, we advance towards purity. Accordingly, our peace and harmony also increase. Eventually, we become positive and motivated at all times.

Thus, the whole interaction with those young students became so rewarding that I thought of sharing it with others.

*****

Cent Percent Negative

Once I was speaking on the subject of 'stress management' at Hardoi. The talk was well received and there was a delighting interaction session at the end of it. The essence of my address was that each one of us is a mixture of positive and negative traits. Our effort should be to increase the positive and the negative will reduce on its own. This is what we call positive attitude or positive thinking. To do so is possible for all of us provided we make an effort. This way the journey of our life should be from darkness to light.

During the interaction, one elderly person rose up and said that he was a cent percent negative person. He wanted to know whether it was possible for him to become positive. For the first time, I had come across a person who considered himself to be a cent percent negative. I responded by saying that according to me no living person can be cent percent negative. If so, either he was not alive or he had some element of positivity. He seemed to agree with this statement. Then I gave him two examples; one of a terminally sick person and the second of a nearly dead plant. In both cases, I said there are chances of survival and no good doctor or gardener will declare them dead as long there is even a trace of life in them. They would certainly try to revive them, though may ultimately fail. Their approach would be to improve the situation bit by bit.

For example, if there is a plant most of the leaves of which have dried up but one or two leaves are still green, it will not be called a dead plant. A good gardener will nurture it with lot of care and hope and if he does so, there are all chances that more new green leaves will grow. The same is true with man also. As long as there is some breath present, there is every chance of recovery. What is required is to have a faith on the laws of Nature. The law of Nature is that it does not disappoint us beyond the point of no return. Even the seeming disappointments of life are for our welfare provided we understand this secret or conspiracy of Nature. There is a silver lining in every disappointment. The need is to identify that silver lining and build upon that bit by bit like a good gardener in case of the plant and the doctor in case of a man. This way, we are our own gardener and our mind is a plant, which has to be nurtured with care.

Certainly there can be no magic in recovery. It has to be a natural process and the fact is that only natural recovery is sustainable. Motivation or positivity, which comes in a shortcut manner, is equally short-lived. What is necessary is to know the principles of our life, to understand them and gradually, let them reflect in our lives. Once on this path, our negativity disappears on its own and we become more and more positive. This is the only way of turning cent percent negative to cent percent positive. However, both the extremes are only an imagination and we must strive to remain as close as possible to cent percent positivity.

The elderly gentleman took my counsel soberly and promised to follow.

*****

Not by Default

We all remain happy and motivated in good times. But no one can say when we may have to face bad times. In fact, life is a series of good and bad times and in a meaningful life they both have to be faced with equanimity. While it is easier to face good times with calmness, it is not so in bad times. The real test of our inner growth is in bad times only. But if we believe that bad times help us to grow internally, we can not only face them with calm, we are also able to win over the adversity. I have a very glaring example of this fact, which I am narrating here.

I had a friend who was a member of an important central service and we were together in the training course at Mussorie in the mid-seventies. Our friendship continued thereafter also and we remained in touch with each other. I found him as one of most smart, competent and good person. He had a very co-operative wife and two bright sons. His life was going on smoothly when bad times shrouded him all of a sudden. Firstly, he contracted a nerve disease, which made him almost immobile as well as speechless. While this disease was in progress his elder son got murdered. The family was contesting this case with a lot of courage but during the course of trial, my friend also passed away. This left his wife alone with her younger son.

One can imagine the severity of the situation for the lady. One day, I visited her in the evening at her residence when she shared with me the challenge she was facing. I had always been her admirer for the courage she had shown till then, but that day she was somewhat nervous. When I was about to leave, she said that at times she is on the verge of breaking down and wants to give up the fight in the face of adverse circumstances.

While a normal person would have done so much earlier, doing so after having gone so far in her fight against adversity did not appear appropriate to me. I also knew that it was only a transient phenomenon and a proper encouragement or support at that stage would give her the strength to fight her full battle. Suddenly, an idea came to my mind which I shared with her. The idea was that adversity should not be allowed to win by default and it should be given a full fight even if we don't feel strong enough to face it. Hearing these words she seemed to have regained her will power and determination to fight the battle till the end. This was amply reflected in her body language also. Few days later, she told me over phone about the positive impact of these words on her.

I was extremely gratified to receive this response. Thereafter, I kept full track of the events which followed in the whole struggle and how boldly and wisely she fought with the negative forces of the system. The final outcome was uncertain till at last the whole nation celebrated the day when she came out as a winner. Certainly, she rose above her adversity and defeated it with her firm resolve.

It will not be correct to presume that merely my words were a source of strength to her. Many help a courageous person and the maximum help comes from Nature. Perhaps in her case, she refused to give a walkover to her adversity and fought with it till the last. The outcome was mainly on account of that fight.

*****

It is Quite Sufficient Sir

Contentment is a great virtue. Though it appears to be a simple word, its understanding and more so living with contentment is one of the most difficult things. The paradox is that the more we acquire, lesser seems to be the level of contentment. India is fortunate in the sense that majority of its people are still content. These are not the people from the higher strata of society but are those whom we consider poor. I have had the privilege of travelling widely in India and came across a large number of people. I have experienced the richness of its poor people closely, which certainly makes me feel proud of my country. Here, I shall share one of my personal experiences in this regard.

I had gone to Mumbai in December 2006 to attend the Global Meet of IITians. I was to stay in the guest house of a public sector undertaking, which was located just adjacent to the airport. The undertaking had made my local travel arrangement also. I reached Mumbai in the forenoon by a morning flight from Bangalore. After check-in at the guest house, I left for the meet. In the evening I was planning to have a quiet dinner at the guest house, but a friend of mine insisted in dining out along with another friend. Thus, we three went to a famous restaurant of Mumbai. I was told that the restaurant was a favourite place for film stars. Though I was not feeling very comfortable with this programme, yet reluctantly I had agreed.

It was already ten in the night when the menu-card came before us. Firstly, it was difficult to identify the items as their names were so unfamiliar and secondly, the prices were beyond my imagination. Somehow, we arrived at an agreed list of items to be ordered and this took another half an hour. By the time we finished our dinner it was well past eleven. The food didn't give any of us much satisfaction though the total bill touched almost a whopping eight thousand rupees. Apart from indicating the level of restaurant, it was also an indication of the income levels in Mumbai. By the time I reached the guest house, the date had changed.

The next thing I suffered was a disturbed sleep after having late dinner. In the morning, the room-bearer brought a cup of tea and appeared to be a good person by his manners, as well as disposition. This was a welcome change and I started talking to him. Apart from many general points I enquired about his family and salary also. His name was Chougale and he belonged to Dharwar district of Karnataka where his family lived. He was alone in Mumbai working in the guest house as a contract employee. He was above forty and appeared quite happy. When asked about salary, he told me that it was two thousand and six hundred rupees per month, which was almost equal to the amount of one meal we had paid for last night. I couldn't believe it and when asked how he could manage himself and his family that was five hundred miles away, he very innocently said, "It is quite sufficient Sir" and went further to explain the break-up. He used to send one thousand rupees to his family, paid six hundred for shelter, three hundred for subsidised food, two hundred for toilet and kept five hundred as pocket money. To him, all this appeared to be very simple.

Silently I saluted this person and gave him a Hindi book of mine as a memento. The next morning he appeared again with a one page compliment about the book, which is still one of my valued possessions. He also gave me a writing pad for my use as a return memento. I was left with no doubt that this person was richer than many wealthy persons living in the financial capital of India.

*****

Right on God

The concept of God is perhaps as ancient as human existence. At all times, God has been conceived in numerous ways. Some consider him to be a very benevolent entity that can be easily pleased by prayers both, genuine or not so genuine while many consider Him to be a tough ruler of the Universe who can inflict any punishment to anyone in anger. Thus, all try to please Him in their own ways. Yet it is difficult to say as to how many trusts Him; forget how many think what is right on God's part.

I have done a lot of contemplation on the subject of God and this has been possible on account of the blessings of many enlightened saints. What I learnt from all of them is that God is the name given to the power of Nature, which is manifested in all its creations both, sentient as well as insentient. This way, we all are essentially divine but unaware of it. The purpose of life is to seek divinity within us so that we regard ourselves as a part of God or in other words, children of God. Once we realise this, all our misgivings about God disappear and we lead a carefree life, like a child in the company of her mother. We can also have a rightful claim on Him provided we obey Him and live in accordance with His laws.

I have an interesting experience to narrate which reinforced my faith in God. As commissioner of Lucknow, a great responsibility was entrusted upon me and my team for arranging unemployment allowance distribution to more than fifty thousand youths coming from different parts of the division. It was a huge task with no previous experience of its kind. It included huge tents, transport arrangement, food arrangements and many other logistics. The time given for this arrangement was very short. The chief minister was personally interested in perfecting the programme and was monitoring it closely. The programme was to be held in the mid of June when there is good likelihood for rain.

Against this background, we all set ourselves for making the arrangements. One problem after the other was coming before us but with a strong team spirit and support from the higher officials, they were being sorted out. Within few days we became confident that the programme would be successful. The only missing point was a rainproof tent could not be arranged for the whole area. The contractor could provide that only for the VIP area. It was his physical limitation and no amount of temptation or threat was of any help.

When the final review of the arrangements was done at the chief secretary's level, this point also came up for discussion. While the chief secretary was convinced that nothing could be done at that point of time and it should be left to chance only, the home secretary took a rigid stand and insisted on the rainproof tent to cover the entire area. He also proposed that if it was not possible, the CM should be advised to change the date. The chief secretary, though not convinced by his proposal, kept silent. However, I took a firm stand. I said that we also have some right on God and it was time to exercise that right.

Immediately, we took the CM into confidence, who understood our limitations and asked us to go ahead with the arrangements. Eventually, it turned out to be a memorable occasion with everything going in perfect way. The chief minister was extremely pleased and praised the whole administration. The fact that it did not rain and nor was it so sunny, was certainly a contribution of God.

*****

Target vs. Goal

Having put in more than three decades in the Indian administrative service, I often feel confused about the process of development in the country. I have almost always been adjudged as an outstanding officer by my superiors. Not only me, most are assessed as very good, if not outstanding. More or less the same is the case with officers of the other services. In the secretariat, which is the centre of governance, there is hardly any exception to this assessment. Individually, we all feel very happy about this achievement and take advantage of it at every opportunity.

The main criterion of this assessment is the fulfilment of the targets set for us during the course of a fixed period, generally a financial year. Towards the end of every financial year, targets fixed by any department are by and large achieved and in most of the cases, the performance is better than the previous year. Going by this fact, by now the nation would have become fully educated, healthy, crime free, clean, employed and prosperous. Every year there is a rise in the number of schools, hospitals, police stations, area sown, productivity, number of tube wells, power generation, road construction so on and so forth. But at the end of all this, we find that the society's grievances against the administration or governance as a whole are on a rise. Everyone feels that the health and education network has deteriorated, there is manifold increase in crime, there is annoying traffic on the roads, there are power shortages, there is lack of sanitation and a host of other problems. And on the face of it, no one can deny these facts.

As commissioner of the Lucknow division, I used to travel a lot in my jurisdiction, which was quite large. I myself noticed this situation closely and at times used to feel pained. One day when I was contemplating over this matter and it occurred to me that while the targets were being achieved by all of us, everyone was missing the goal. One reason according to me is that while we applied the entire mind to achieve the target there is hardly any application of heart in our work. Unless we do our work with head and heart both, the true purpose of our work is never achieved. Secondly, our individual growth appears to be enough to us. While it may be true in the short-run but if we work for cross purposes, everyone ends up losing in the long-run. This is what seems to have happened today.

I conveyed my feelings to all senior officers working with me in the form of a letter, which was very much appreciated. I don't know how many of them went beyond appreciation but it is my conviction that unless the goal of development is achieved, mere achievement of targets has no meaning. In other words, unless there is rise in 'gross national happiness' or 'per capita happiness', rise in 'gross national income' or 'per capita income' is meaningless. This is possible only when we pay attention to both, the outer as well as the inner development of the society, and this requires the employment of both, our 'head' and 'heart' in work. The same is true for life also. If the goal of life is to be achieved, we must not only be smart but also good.

*****

How Poor We Are

In this write-up, I am sharing a story I read somewhere and which gives a great message. The story goes like this:

There was a rich man who used to live in a luxurious house with his family. The man had risen from a humble background and had seen poverty closely. But his children were never exposed to poverty and grew in luxury. Once this rich man decided to expose his children to poverty and arranged their stay in a village at a poor man's house for few days. He deliberately didn't accompany them so that they could wander around freely. Accordingly, the children were sent to the village.

The children enjoyed their village stay thoroughly. For the first time, they had a first-hand experience of openness. They slept there in the open, as the visit was during their summer holidays. The weather was clear and so there were shining stars in the sky during the night. There were a number of cattle and street dogs in the village, which used to roam around. The food was cooked on wooden fire in the open. There were big open fields all around the village where children used to play. In all, they enjoyed their stay in the village and returned to the city after few days.

On their return, their father asked them whether they had realised what poverty was. The children very fondly answered in the affirmative and went on to describe their assessment of poverty. They said that the bedroom in the village was so big that it had no boundary wall. The roof was also equally big. While the ceiling of their bedroom had only few lamps, the village roof had countless lamps. The same case was with the kitchen size and the number of cattle. In the city they had only one pet while there were a number of pets in the village. Summing up the whole visit, the children unanimously concluded that now they had realised how poor they were as compared to the village people.

The morale of the story is so obvious. Richness is a state of mind and as long as we consider ourselves to be a part of Nature, we are rich. Continuous exposure to worldly definition of riches makes us narrow-minded and we become blind to the wealth of Nature. Children, who are closer to Nature, are still able to appreciate natural beauty and therefore, felt poor when exposed to natural surroundings. The same situation however, was perceived differently by the grown-up parents for whom personal richness was the only criterion of wealth.

Let us therefore feel rich in the lap of Nature because eventually, all our so-called possessions are in the mind and their actual ownership lies with Nature.

*****

Cosmic Vision

It is said that vision is the art of seeing invisible things. Where there is no vision, people perish. Therefore, every society needs some visionaries if it has to survive and prosper in the long-run. India has been fortunate in the sense that this country has produced a large number of great men and women. They thought of much ahead of their times and gave a rich heritage to this country. India was known for its values, cultural heritage and spiritual strength. British rulers saw this as a threat to their rule as was mentioned by Lord Macaulay, in the British parliament, in February 1835. As a result, a new education policy was framed which gradually made our people short-sighted, a legacy which still continues to a great extent.

Indian independence has now become six decades old. The nation has grown in many areas. The advance made in the field of science and technology has been a matter of pride and has brought glory to India and throughout the world. But there are many areas of shame, which if not addressed urgently; they will wipe out all that we have gained from our economic progress. For this, the nation's vision has to expand. Our people in general and rulers in particular have to rise above their individual narrow interests. Be they politicians or administrators or media or judiciary, all need this expansion maybe in varying degrees and the beginning has to be made by oneself. I have done some contemplation in this regard, which I am sharing here.

The social variation in this country is widespread and the vision of the people also varies accordingly. There are a large number of poor persons who are bogged down in their day to day existence. As a result, they cannot think beyond their daily lives. Their worry is whether they will be able to get employment, food, shelter or other essential requirements of life everyday. These are the people who fall in the category of Below Poverty Line (BPL). Despite all efforts, there is hardly any visible change in their number or condition. Then there are people who are better placed and have a job or work in their hands. Their vision is almost confined to one year. All they want is to increase their profit year after year. If they are able to achieve this objective, they are satisfied.

The next category is that of the politicians who at the best think of the five-year span and want to win the next election irrespective of the means adopted by them. Now, even the five-year span is shortened by mid-term elections. Even during this period, many of them change their loyalties, if it helps in winning the next election. Very few of the politicians take a large view of their profession and think of a generation. Fortunately, India has had such politicians and I place them in the category of 'statesmen'. They passed on their values and conviction to the next generation. Such leaders are remembered for a long time and their vision covers a span of about 25 years.

Higher than the category of a 'statesmen' are those who think of many generations and have a vision span of say 100 years. Persons like Ram Mohan Roy, Tagore, Baba Amte, Mahatma Gandhi, Abul Kalam Azad, Ambedkar fall in this category. They bring out social reform in the society, which stays for many generations. We may call them visionaries. There is still a higher category of persons whose presence is felt for thousands of years. I place them in the category of incarnations. Such persons are Ram, Krishna, Christ, Guru Nanak, Hazrat Mohammad and few others who fall in this category. They take birth whenever deterioration in the society falls beyond a critical point.

Lastly, there is only one entity whose vision is for eternity and such vision can be classified as 'cosmic vision'. This person is none but God himself. The human existence is only few thousand years old but the cosmos is ageless. It has existed for millions of years and will continue to exist for as many years.

Our effort should be to expand our vision continuously and from 'daily' to 'cosmic' or 'eternal'. It is possible for all human beings and that is eventually the goal of human life. Let us, therefore, strive to achieve cosmic vision or be as near to it as possible.

*****

Crime vs. Sin

The understanding of the difference between crime and sin is useful for positive living. In the absence of this, most of us often question the fairness of God and tend to follow a path of evil. I have done some contemplation on this subject, which I am sharing here.

Like any other living creature, the human being is also a product of Nature. But man is unique in the sense that he has been endowed with the power of thinking as well as discrimination. With the help of these two powerful tools, he can either make himself a saint or a devil, depending upon their use. Nature expects him to use these powers in a positive manner and if he does so, he becomes a virtuous person. On the contrary, negative use of these powers makes him a sinful person. Thus, when we break a Nature-made or in other words, God-made law we commit a sin. For example, God expects us to love each other and if one hates others, he commits a sin. Similarly, when we hurt others, lose our temper, boost our ego, don't help a person in trouble, etc., we break the law of Nature and commit a sin.

Nature has a perfect arrangement of punishing sin and rewarding virtue. No external agency is required to do this job. When we practice virtue, the inner joy obtained as a result of the same is in itself a great reward. It changes our body chemistry in such a manner that there is an overall positive effect on our body, mind, intellect and spirit. There may not be any monetary evaluation for this reward, but we get priceless joy. Similarly, when we commit a sin there is change in our body chemistry, which brings negative effect on our body, mind, intellect and spirit. In this case, there is loss of joy, which again cannot be measured in monetary terms. In this way, being virtuous is in itself our reward and same is the case with sin. Someone has very rightly said:

"We are not punished for our sins, but by our sins."

A wise person will therefore be virtuous by choice and not by compulsion. It is also true that this law of Nature never fails.

On the other hand, crime is a violation of man-made laws. Man being a social entity, has to follow some man-made laws for the smooth running of the society. Better is the compliance of these laws, more civilised will be the society. For this, there is provision of reward and punishments through the judicial administrative process. Quite often justice is not administered correctly due to various reasons and many criminals don't get punished. In such a situation, most of us blame God and feel that He is not judicious.

In order to forego this impression, we shall have to understand that all crimes are not sins and similarly all sins may not necessarily be crimes. God punishes us only for our sins and if a crime falls in the category of sin also, it would certainly be punished by Nature. But, if a crime does not fall in the category of sin, Nature will not punish us and the punishment has to be imparted by society only. In that case, it is a human failure for which God can not be blamed, as He has already equipped us with the power of intelligence and discrimination.

Therefore, we all should live in accordance with the laws of Nature, as well as of the society so that we neither commit a sin nor a crime.

*****

Rich Man's Diwali

India is a country of many festivals, celebrated by various communities in various parts of the country. Going by the Hindu calendar, almost each day is a festival in one way or the other. However, major festivals of various communities are few and celebrated with great joy and participation.

One of the major festivals of Hindus is Diwali. It is a festival of light and sweets. It is celebrated on the dark night of Kartika and generally falls in the second half of October or first half of November. On this day, Lord Rama had returned to his kingdom of Ayodhya after completing 14 years of exile and destroying countless demons during this period, including the powerful Ravana. Thus, this festival signifies the victory of light over darkness and of virtue over evil. That is why lamps are lit all around and sweets are distributed among friends and relatives. People visit each other carrying sweets and gifts as a mark of goodwill. They also enjoy fireworks and crackers in the night. With materialism on the rise, this exchange of sweets and gifts has assumed huge proportions and has become an expensive affair. Even the fireworks and crackers have become very expensive. In this way, this great festival has gradually become an extravaganza for the rich while the poor try to celebrate it with their limited resources, quite often envying the rich.

I have been watching this phenomenon since my childhood. I still remember the joy of buying few kilograms of sweets in an open utensil in the company of my father.

In those days, there was no packing and the prices were low. So we could buy lot of sweets within one hundred rupees and thereafter distributed them among friends. Not only this, eating sweets was a matter of great joy and each piece was enjoyed thoroughly. The whole community participated in each other's celebration with hardly any comparisons.

Today, things have changed greatly. I have watched this change more keenly as a member of the Indian administrative services. While in the initial years of the service one pack of sweets was enough to show respect, currently it has no meaning. A good number of people, particularly the neo-rich, feel that the respect is directly proportional to the price of gifts or the number of packets. They load their expensive cars with expensive sweets and gifts and pass them on to those whose pleasure can benefit them or displeasure may harm them. Quite often, their Diwali passes in running around the town or sending couriers to other towns. As a member of the Indian administrative services, I have also been a beneficiary of their charity. It is a different matter that most of them developed a personal relationship in due course and I share their gifts with many others.

But what about the rich man's own Diwali? While they distribute lots of sweets and dry fruits, I have not seen any of them enjoying even one piece of sweet. Whenever they are offered sweets, they beg to be excused with folded hands and say that in Diwali sweets were a taboo for them. And I very amusingly watch this, thinking that if they cannot even see sweets in Diwali, what kind of Diwali would they be celebrating. On the other hand, the lesser mortals enjoy sweets thoroughly and anything passed onto them is a matter of joy for the giver as well as the receiver. At least from this point of view, Diwali has no meaning for the rich; it is the poor who enjoy the festival most. Surely, the poor need not envy the rich for their extravaganza.

*****

Diversity in Unity

India is a vast country with mind-boggling variety in term of its people, food, dress, customs, language, social practices and ethos. Though I have been very fortunate to have widely travelled all across the country, I have no hesitation in admitting that my knowledge about this country is not even a tip of the iceberg. All that I have realised as a result of this travelling is that the diversity of our country is overall a matter of strength and not weakness. Those who feel otherwise are mistaken and need to understand the reasons of India's unity in such diversity.

While one comes across many write-ups, books, lectures, etc., on this subject, the one which gave me maximum conviction and clarity was the one by Mr Shashi Tharoor, an ex-UN diplomat from India. The occasion was the IITian Meet at Mumbai in December 2006 in which about 5000 delegates participated from various parts of the world. He beautifully explained the diversity of India in respect of all the parameters and also the factors, which bind Indians together. While we quarrel with each other on several local issues, when it comes to a larger national interest, we show solidarity with each other. This is something which is not easily found elsewhere. While this contention may be a matter of debate among some, the fact can not be denied that India has survived many crises and not only survived but rose above them. Whether it a matter of communal riots, natural calamities, accidents or terrorist activities, the nation has by and large faced them gracefully. If so, it becomes a matter of contemplation as to what is the underlying strength behind this.

Mr Tharoor tried to explain this very convincingly. He said that in India we are not to seek unity in diversity but the other way round. India basically is one culture or a united nation with lot of diversity. Our plurality emerges from a single composite culture and therefore unity is our primary nature. What is to be appreciated is the diversity in its unity instead of seeing unity in its diversity. This very fact is the secret of India's survival through the ages.

The question arises that if such is our underlying strength, why do we look so disjointed in our day to day existence. It has been said that one Indian is equal to ten Japanese but ten Indians are equal to one Japanese. There is sense in this statement. While individually Indians perform very well, collectively we loose our strength. This is perhaps due to the long period of foreign rule in India, as a result of which we seem to have forgotten our strength. All these foreign rules tried to attack our ancient heritage and culture and in the process divided our society. The present state of affairs is a legacy of the same.

India has now completed six decades of its independence. This is a long period. We are also marching towards development in many areas and have made our name in the world. Yet there are many gaps and the major one is the lack of patriotism in our people. We still see the governance as some thing alien to us and all our anger is directed towards governmental machinery. This is a losing proposition for all. We must realise now that we are the makers of our destiny and no outside help can do it. And if we are able to realise this fact and act on it, then only the underlying unity of India will prove to be its real strength.

*****

Spiritual Journey

While I was studying at the University of Roorkee (now an IIT) during 1966 to 1970, our dean of students was a professor named Jagdish Narain. He was from the civil engineering department and was known in his field, academically. He was a reserved kind of person and had little interaction with students. As a result, he was not very popular as dean of the University. During his period, there was some agitation by the students, which he did not handle firmly and the situation turned ugly. At that time as well as in retrospect, I always felt that had he reprimanded us at the right point of time, the situation would not have become ugly.

With this background, I left the University in the year 1970. Though I kept in contact with the University, there were no personal contacts with Prof. Jagdish Narain. After few years, he retired from there and I never heard of him after that. It was only in the year 2006 when a meet of distinguished IITians was organised in Delhi, that I saw him there. We both were attending the meet and when I introduced myself to him, I learnt that he was living in Sai Baba's *ashram* at Puttaparthy as his devotee. This was something very surprising to me and I became keen to know about his journey to spirituality. Going by his ways at the University, it was difficult for me to believe that he could turn so spiritual, though I myself had become so. Anyway, there was no occasion to talk on this issue during the meet and the matter ended there.

Only few months later in December 2006, I had gone to Bangalore for two days and on one of these days, I planned a visit to Puttaparthy along with a friend of mine. I had been wishing to visit this place for long and this time, it worked out smoothly. A friend of mine in Hyderabad made the necessary arrangement for the Baba's *darshan* at Puttaparthy and I took my seat at a prominent place quite before Baba was to arrive for the *darshan*. While waiting there, I was remembering Prof. Jagdish Narain and silently expecting him also to arrive there. And to my pleasant surprise, I immediately noticed him coming there slowly and taking his seat just adjacent to him. Since he had met me only few months back, he recognised me at once and I was also very happy at this divine coincidence.

Incidentally, Baba's arrival got delayed and so I got sometime to talk to him. This time I could ask him about his journey to spirituality and he narrated it very affectionately. He told me that few years after his retirement he had come to the *ashram* in connection with a technical advice on building matter. As soon as he met Baba here, a mutual bond got established and thereafter he became a devotee of Baba. Not only that, he also shifted to the *ashram* and started living here. He himself was surprised by this sudden change in him but he had no doubt that now, he was on the right path. This interaction of mine with Prof. Jagdish Narain gave me great joy and I fondly remember it frequently.

This is what life is. Our ultimate aim is to know our spiritual nature and to realise it. Nobody knows when and how it will happen but there is no doubt that one day it has to happen. Fortunate are those who get an early opportunity. Let us all strive for it.

*****

Everything is All right

In the mid-nineties, I came across a book titled *'Dew Drops on a Lotus Leaf'* written by Sri Ramalu, also known as Sri Ram of Andhra Pradesh. This book was a collection of letters from seekers to Sri Ram and their replies by him. The letters as well as the replies were full of depth and more so the latter. This created a wish in me to meet him. The above mentioned book was published by my own book's publisher and so I could get his details from him.

The opportunity to meet Sri Ramalu came soon in early 1998 when I was appointed as an observer for the parliamentary elections in Andhra Pradesh. Sri Ramalu was then working in a polytechnic at Adilabad, a town nearly 200 kilometres from Hyderabad. He was a lecturer in the department of English. An IPS friend of mine arranged my visit to Adilabad and I got an opportunity of spending few hours with Sri Ramalu. It was a very sublime meeting and we both liked the company of each other. I also noticed that Sri Ramalu was treated almost as a living God by those who knew him closely.

Soon after this, I received a letter from Sri Ramalu and apart from mentioning our meeting he gave a very deep message through that letter which I am sharing here. In one paragraph of the letter Sri Ramalu raised a question about 'faith'. Normally, all those who have faith in God believe that everything will be all right in their lives. While apparently there is nothing wrong with this definition of 'faith', Sri Ramalu said that it was not faith but the lack of it.

He explained further that when we say that the future is going to be all right, indirectly it implies that perhaps, the present is not all right. Since we live only in the present, according to this definition of faith the feeling of being all right becomes only an imagination of future, which soon becomes the present. Thus, it becomes a chasing game that goes on throughout our life.

He further explained that the correct definition of faith is, 'everything is all right'. As a matter of fact both definitions are the same; the difference is in the way of looking at it. What is the future today becomes present in due course. So if we shift our focus little backwards, we can always believe that the present is the best possible as of now. Our endeavour would then become to make the future better by working for it today.

Viewed from a different perspective, there can be no denial to the fact that the present can not be better that what it is. It could be; had we thought of it yesterday and tomorrow can be better if we think of it today. But the present remains as it is and no purpose is served by complaining about it, even if there is reason to complain about it. Therefore, a person of true faith never laments about the present, never regrets the past and never worries for the future. He has complete faith on the laws of Nature and does his best in all circumstances. For him, everything is all right at all times and he lives in perfect tune with Nature. Accordingly, for Sri Ramalu, this is what true faith is.

*****

Wedding Lunch

Once, I received an invitation from a good friend of mine for his son's marriage. The friend belonged to Gorakhpur, while I was at Lucknow. Our friendship had developed during my posting at Gorakhpur and it continued thereon. My friend's family is an old traditional family of Gorakhpur and at that time was considered to be the richest in Gorakhpur. Not that alone, the family was also known for its culture and values. Any interaction with the family used to be very graceful and gratifying. That is why the association continued even long after my transfer from Gorakhpur.

The marriage ceremony was to be held in Lucknow and he was his only son. I was therefore, keenly looking forward to attend the same. The ceremony was to be held in a star hotel of Lucknow and the reception was at lunch time. So I planned to reach there directly from the office, while my wife was to join us from home. We both reached there in time and as indicated on the invitation card. After reaching the venue, we found that the marriage procession was still away from the venue and it was expected to reach in about half an hour. Though it made us a bit uneasy, there was no option but to wait. My problem was the office timings and also my sugar level, as I am diabetic. However, we could afford to wait for about half an hour.

But to our surprise for the every half an hour we waited, there was no indication of the marriage procession reaching the venue. Though it was then visible, most of the members in the procession were busy dancing and merry-making. All this made me, in particular, very upset and I requested those present at the venue to arrange for my lunch. Perhaps there were no instructions to this effect and so they refused to oblige. Meanwhile, my sugar level started going down and I was getting late for office. In this situation, I had no option but to arrange for my own lunch.

So I went to the hotel restaurant and ordered my lunch. Since I have a less appetite, a mini-lunch sufficed for me but even that costed me about two hundred rupees in that hotel. Fortunately, my wife had no such problem and she decided to stay back and attend the reception. After lunch, I left the venue and reached my office. Just then the procession had also reached the venue but I deliberately avoided it, to save my friend from any embarrassment.

My wife of course, attended the marriage and met my friend also but no serious mention was made of my reaching there as well as leaving. In the rush, even my friend did not come to know about it. The matter came up only after few months when our friend visited us at our home in Lucknow. At that time, he only mentioned that I was not seen during his son's marriage. Then I narrated him the whole incident, not by way of any complaint but more so to put forth the point that how modern expensive marriages create inconvenience to real well-wishers. He took the narration in a positive manner and expressed his sincere regret, which of course was not my purpose. My only response was that by paying for my own lunch at his son's marriage he owed me a debt, which I would recover at my own convenience.

*****

Backbone of India

Perhaps very few know that Lord Macaulay in his address to the British Parliament on the 2nd of February 1835, made the following statement:

"I have travelled across the length and breadth of India and have not seen one person who is a beggar, who is a thief. Such wealth I have seen in this country, such high moral values, people of such calibre, that I do not think we would ever conquer this country, unless we break the very backbone of this nation, which is her spiritual and cultural heritage. And, therefore, I propose that we replace her old and ancient education system, her culture, for if the Indians think all that is foreign and English is good and greater than their own, they will lose their self-esteem, their native culture and they will become what we want them, a truly dominated nation."

When I first came to know of this statement, my apprehensions about the British strategy of ruling India got confirmed. During my twelve weeks stay in the UK for a training programme way back in 1990, I had been contemplating over the point as to how a small nation like Britain could rule over countries like India and many others. My apprehension at that time was that the British tried to split the nation ruled by them by polluting its culture and this is what they did in India also.

It is a fact that despite many centuries of foreign rule, India was still a culturally and materially rich nation. That is why it was known as the 'Golden Bird' at that time and this finds proof in the above statement of Lord Macaulay. This statement amply proves that our moral values, cultural heritage and spiritual wisdom were a matter of envy even for powerful nations like Britain. Britishers found it so formidable that they planned to break it first before they could think of ruling India for a long time. As a result, they intruded into our culture through the route of education and succeeded to a great extent. The legacy of this system continues till today.

India's freedom is now more than sixty years old. During this period, we made tremendous progress in many fields. But to say that India is a developed and powerful nation in a true sense is wrong. A vast majority of the Indian population is still struggling for a dignified survival. The progress of a section of population can not be called the progress of the nation. Our human development index is dismally low. With the rise in industrial growth rate, we are slipping in our integrity score, which stands at 3.4 on a scale of 10. This puts India at the 85th rank among 180 countries. Our education, health, sanitation and human rights parameters are poor and despite deployment of huge funds, the situation is not improving appreciably.

This is a matter of great concern for all those who are patriotic in a true sense. Lot of debate and serious thinking is going on in this regard. It is now being realised that the answer to these problems also lies in the statement of Lord Macaulay. Once again, we have to understand the depth of our ancient values and spiritual wisdom, which have no direct conflict with the modern times. At best, they need to be interpreted in the face of scientific and technological progress. If we are able to do so, India can once again achieve its place, it used to occupy once upon a time. Time has now come to pay serious attention to our national values in order to restore them. Only then, the backbone of India will become straight and strong.

*****

No Help is Small

In a mutually dependent society, we all need each other's help and no good life can be imagined without it. The sole purpose of having friends and relatives is to seek their help or to extend our help to them whenever such a need arises. At the same time, it is also a fact that only close relatives and friends turn into enemies when such obligations are not met as per our or their expectations. Therefore, it is essential to understand what precaution is required to avoid this situation.

Many years back, I was attending a seminar of a famous motivator, Shiv Khera in Nainital. During the course of one discussion, he touched upon this aspect and I drew a very important lesson out of that. He mentioned that, most of us are very casual in seeking help and take it for granted. Quite often we seek help from other's just in a by the way manner. Such help is sought in a manner as if no effort is called on the part of the helper and further, as if it is an obligation on his part to help. Moreover, for seeking such help, a lot of time is wasted in irrelevant talks. What Mr Shiv Khera meant was that if we seek help from others, howsoever small it may be, it should be sought with great politeness and without beating around the bush. Also, the difficulty or the dilemma of the person should be kept in mind and so a margin should be given to him to apply his discretion. When it is not done, sooner or later it affects our relationship and no wonder a point may reach when such relationship turns into enmity.

I myself have experienced this difficulty in my long career of administrative service. Since we have access to almost all areas of public administration, help is sought by a large number of people. Quite often, they don't come to the point immediately and waste time talking about other things. It is so annoying that one feels like snubbing the person concerned. Over that, they feel it requires no effort on our part and judge our sincerity, competence or influence on the basis of the outcome. This affects the relationship further. My own approach is to try my best in case of a genuine need, but generally I am immune to the outcome and don't get overjoyed on positive outcomes nor get upset on negative ones. But certainly, it is not the case with the person who seeks help.

The message of this discussion is that when we seek help from others, we have to be very wise. The point to be kept in mind is that, putting a demand or expectation is very easy but it requires quite an effort to act on that. So many factors play their role in when something happens or does not happen. First of all, one's expectation should be genuine and not unduly selfish. Secondly, the limitation of the other person should be understood and thirdly, it should not be placed as a matter of right but only as a prayer. The fact is that no help is small and each requires commitment, energy and sincerity. If nothing else, all these should be respected even if the outcome is not positive. If we take care of these factors, not only will the chances of a positive outcome increase, the chances of a souring relationship also decrease greatly.

*****

Sauce and Rice

J visited South Korea for the first time in the year 1995. Before that, I had been to Japan twice in 1988 and 1989. At that time, Japan was considered to be the most developed nation of the east and South Korea was only trying to come up. It was no match to Japan and there appeared to be no chance also of it becoming so. But that was exactly what had happened by the year 1995 and the possibility of South Korea leaving behind Japan was also not being ruled out. Against this background, the visit to South Korea had become very enlightening as well as inspiring. One of the memorable examples was the visit to the POSCO steel plant, where our delegation was received very warmly. The environment of the plant was so good that we felt like we were going around in a park.

During the course of this visit, the Indian ambassador in South Korea had hosted us a dinner. While we were talking about many good things about the country, the ambassador told us that the whole development of South Korea was a matter of only thirty years. Before that, it was a poor country and the people there could merely manage to afford only the staple food. The prevalent saying there was that, the people at that time had only one variation in their menu, and it was sauce (*chatni*) and rice (*chawal*) at lunch time and rice and sauce at dinner time. This was all they knew about food. From that stage, South Korea had achieved the status of one of the most developed nation within a span of three decades.

This narration by the ambassador was not only interesting but inspiring also. He also mentioned that the main reason behind this progress was the committed leadership in the country. It was not only the vision of the leader but competence coupled with discipline of the people on account of faith as well as fear. This was another message for us. Thereafter, I had the chance of visiting few more countries in the east. The secret of success everywhere was the same. The people have to become a part of the development process and it happens, only when there is competent, committed and firm leadership.

India is now a nation of more than one million but there is dearth of leadership, which meets the above criterion. Still, it will be wrong to say that we stand no chance. After all, our country has produced a leader like Mahatma Gandhi, whose philosophy is now being considered relevant all across the globe. The fact that we have not tried to understand him correctly, what to say of following him, is perhaps the main reason behind the delay of our progress. But delays are not denials. Our country is fortunate to have much better resources and certainly our people's staple food is *dal* (lentil) and *chawal* (rice), better than the Koreans at the beginning of their development. Let us learn from the experiences of such countries.

*****

Catholic or Protestant

Once, I was on an official visit to Mumbai and was staying in my departmental guest house located in Pali Hill area. In the same building, my regional officer also used to stay with his family. Even during tours, I am in the habit of going for a morning walk. This is not only refreshing but also gives a lot of insight into the local area. In that visit, my regional manager advised me to go a nearby park for a morning walk and accompanied me to that place. I found the place very well maintained and enjoyed walking there. There was a nominal admission fee, which was being used for its maintenance by a citizen's society.

As we came out of the park after a refreshing walk, I saw a church adjacent to it. Since I like to visit worship places of different religions, I advised my colleague to go inside the church to offer our prayers. He himself being a religious person agreed to my suggestion and we both went inside the church. At that time, the morning prayers were about to conclude and so we also took our seats at the back. After the prayers, all those present there were proceeding towards the statue of Christ for seeking His blessings. We also stood in the queue in order to seek His blessings from near.

As we were moving towards the statue of Christ, at a point we were stopped and were asked whether we were Catholics or Protestants. I never see a religion from this viewpoint and so apart from being ignorant I am also opposed to this kind of man-made distinction. So my response was that we were neither of them but were only human beings. The person who made the enquiry from us was perhaps not used to this kind of an answer. His prompt response was that in that case we were not allowed to go further. Respecting the tradition of the church, we didn't mind and came out of the church after offering our prayers from a distance only. Thus, the matter ended there itself.

However, his enquiry and response to my answer still keeps coming to my mind. Which religion can be superior to a good human being but perhaps all religious have drawn their boundaries may be in varying degrees. I am not sure whether this is in the larger interest or not, but if we go by the definition of spirituality, it is the infinite expansion of the mind. Viewed from that perspective, such boundaries are certainly not in a larger interest.

In the era we are living today, there is a need for rethinking on such restrictions, irrespective of the religion. I must also add that the above experience has in no way affected my reverence towards any religion.

*****

Nam Sankirtan

*I*n August 2004, I had gone to Kerala to visit my spiritual master Swami Bhoomananda Tirtha whose *ashram* is located at Trichur. It has beautiful surroundings and the entire area is lush green. The visit was soon after the Guru Poornima celebrations were over but one activity of 'Daan-Satra' was still on. This is a very sublime activity in which poor families of the nearby villages are provided some help in the form of cash, rice and clothes. Poor people of the area look forward to this occasion with a lot of fondness. For them, it is more of a blessing than help. *Swamiji* also ensures that this distribution ceremony is conducted with perfection and humility.

During my above visit, *Swamiji* took me along with him for one such distribution function. Firstly, the drive through the Kerala villages was in itself a great joy. Soon, we reached the village where the function was arranged. People had already gathered there waiting eagerly for *Swamiji's* arrival. Many of them were very poor but all were looking happy. In the whole gathering, there was hardly anyone who could communicate in a language other than Malayalam. Therefore, the only person I could communicate with was *Swamiji*. Still, I could read the body language of all and my inference was that the proceedings were very sublime making everyone happy.

As soon as the distribution part was over, it was time for chanting, *Swamiji* himself initiated the process by chanting '*Hare Krishna Hare Krishna, Krishna Krishna Hare*

Hare'. And to my surprise, every one in the gathering joined in chorus with correct pronunciation. This was something new to me and gave me a lot of pleasure. Earlier, I had noticed the similar thing in Andhra Pradesh as well as in Tamil Nadu, where I had been on election duties.

This set me thinking about the efforts, which must have gone into propagating the names of our Gods throughout the length and breadth of the country. This happened thousands of years back, when there were hardly any means of communication and travel. Today, despite all these means and lot of investment, such campaigns are only short-lived and people soon forget all that is conveyed through such campaigns. On the contrary, what our great saints and seers spread in temples and pilgrimages, still remains in our memory. Surely, their message is directed to the heart rather than to the head. This is the difference between the spiritual and the secular.

*****

I Will Buy It

One small incident during my visit to Japan in the year 1988 still occupies my mind. At that time, I was posted as managing director of UP Export Corporation and had gone to Japan to participate in an exhibition at Kobe. My commercial manager was accompanying me and we had displayed a large number of handloom and handicraft items from Uttar Pradesh. They included some silk scarves from Varanasi. The exhibition was organised by the Trade Development Authority of India, which had provided us the necessary infrastructure including the interpreter.

Our interpreter was a young Japanese girl aged about 14. She was cute and well-mannered. We found her services very satisfactory. During the course of the exhibition, we noticed that her attention was repeatedly falling on a silk scarf displayed there. It was obvious that she liked it and perhaps wanted to possess it. One day, when I asked her whether she liked it, she answered in the affirmative and also added that she would like to buy the same after the exhibition was over. Over this, I offered it as a gift from our side. I was surprised with her response to this offer. She firmly said that since she was earning her wages, in no case she would accept it as a gift. Moreover, it was against the tradition of her country, she added further.

For us, it was a pleasant experience. We wondered over the sense of pride at such a young age, for one's own as well as for the country's dignity. While we deeply appreciated her stand, it was equally wrong on our part to accept money for a sample, which was not meant for sale. But she was not agreeing with our plea and kept on insisting on payment. The matter went on like this till the last day of the exhibition.

When it came to winding up the display, I offered her the scarf as a gift and gave the plea that it was against the tradition of our country too to sell something, which was not meant for sale. We also pleaded that it would give us immense pleasure if she accepted it as a gift. She was convinced with our plea and very reluctantly, as well as gratefully, accepted the same.

Quite often, I remember the gesture of that young girl. We were left with no doubt that great nations are due to great people and unless they display character in thoughts, words and actions, no amount of economic growth can make a nation great.

*****

Old Newspapers

I have a sister who is about ten years elder to me. She brought me up in my childhood days and took care of me like a mother. Even after her marriage (which was at the age of 16), I spent few years with her and had my primary education at the place of my brother-in-law's posting. Thereafter, we have been visiting each other very frequently. She has been a very good home manager and always took good care of all visitors within her means.

One event, which I usually noticed with her, was the disposal of old newspapers. The deal between the hawker and her used to fail on many accounts. Sometimes it was over rate, sometimes over the weighing balance and sometimes over some other issue. As a result, quite often the old newspapers were brought out of the house and then taken back. The deal used to conclude only after many such exercises. Seeing this, I always used to feel that in the whole process, the pain was more than the gain but my sister would not listen to any advice in the matter.

In due course, as she became mature and saw life in a larger perspective, she used to realise the waste of energy in this exercise. At the same time, nature brought me on the spiritual path and she started looking at me as her spiritual guide. Before this, she was a very sentimental woman who was prepared to sacrifice anything for others but at the same time felt sad if her sentiments were not appreciated or responded adequately. Once she realised that one should live with a sense of detachment while doing one's duty sincerely, the texture of her life changed. Thereafter, she stopped wasting her energy in trivial matters like disposal of old newspapers.

The message of this small narration is deep. Most of us waste a lot of energy firstly in acquiring things and then in getting rid of them. The wisdom lies in applying moderation in both the areas. One should understand the essential nature of physical acquisitions. They come to us only to go. Therefore, only optimum acquisition should be our target and their going away also should not bother us unduly. While it is applicable to objects, it is equally important for our relationships. One should, therefore, live like an observer in this world. Since then my sister is a much happier person and does not waste her energy for petty issues such as the disposal of old newspapers.

*****

Breaking Steel Ingots

*M*andi Gobind Garh is a medium town of Punjab known for its steel industry. The entrepreneurship of this place is appreciated all over the country. The industry here is engaged in almost all activities related to steel. I had the opportunity of visiting this town several times, when I was posted in the department of steel during the year 1991-96. During one of the visits, I observed a very interesting process of breaking steel ingots (big steel blocks coming directly from the steel plants).

In this process, steel ingots were first marked by a chisel and hammered at a line around the periphery of the ingot from where it was to be broken. This was normally done in the evening and the ingot was then left open during the night. In the morning, the portion to be broken was hammered repeatedly. During the course of this process, the ingot used to break in one hammering. The beauty of the operation was that the ingot broke in one hammering only, but it was not certain in which one would it happen. Sometimes, it could be fifth or tenth or even seventy-fifth. I was told that in some rare case it happened in the first hammering also.

Even with my mechanical engineering background, I could not clearly understand the science of this process. But certainly, I tried to give it a philosophical meaning. The message I got from this was that when we have a goal before us, our duty is to proceed in the direction of its achievement. If we strive with full sincerity and zeal, the goal would certainly be achieved. It is a different matter whether it is achieved after one failure or more than one failure. If we achieve our target after few failures, it would not be proper to say that the failures before success had no purpose. In a way, each failure is a step towards success provided we don't give up after failure.

I also often compare this process with our freedom struggle, which began in the year 1857. To begin with, it was felt that independence was just round the corner but it was not to be so. It took us 90 years to get the freedom. In the meantime, thousands gave their lives for its sake. But to say that their sacrifice had no role in achieving the freedom will be totally wrong. In fact, each sacrifice was a definite step in the direction of freedom and should be acknowledged with gratefulness.

Let us live life in this spirit and if we do so, we enjoy our failures too, as much as we do the same for our successes.

*****

Universal Consciousness

In the mid-eighties, I came across a saint known as Swami Shyam at Kanpur. He had come there to stay with a close friend of mine, who was his disciple. I was quite influenced by his discourse and developed a liking for him. Swami Shyam was living in Kullu town of Himachal Pradesh, where he had a well established *ashram*. Most of his disciples were from the western countries and belonged to the upper class of the society. Many of them were scientists of great repute. After meeting him, I had developed a wish of visiting his *ashram* also.

This opportunity came to me in November 1993, when I was appointed as an election observer for the Himachal assembly election. At that time, I was posted at Delhi and the district allotted to me was Manali, which was adjacent to Kullu. For reaching there, I had to first fly to Kullu and then travel by road. I had to visit the district of my duty three times and twice I visited Swami Shyam's ashram at Kullu. Fortunately, *Swamiji* was at his *ashram* at that time and so I could interact with him closely. Once I had an enlightening interaction with his disciples also, which was an honour for me, as *Swamiji* had desired me to address them.

During my second visit to the *ashram*, I had a personal interaction with *Swamiji*. At that time, the Kabir Peace Mission, which had been founded only three years back, was in its formative stage and I was crystallising my agenda to serve the society through this mission. Keeping this in mind, I put a question to *Swamiji* as to how one could serve the society best. To this, *Swamiji* responded in a very pragmatic manner and gave me a message, which I carry till today. I am sharing the same here.

Swamiji said that in true spiritual sense, it is ignorance to think of serving others. All our good pursuits are eventually to help us only. Since each one of us is a part of the cosmic consciousness, our actions have an effect on it. When we transmit positive energy to this universal consciousness, all get benefited including ourselves. Same is the case, when we transmit negative energy to it. So the best way to serve others is to raise our own consciousness level, so that the level of universal consciousness also goes up. This in the process serves all. This raising of consciousness can be done both, at the physical and mental level. He also said that the service at the mental level is superior to the physical level service. Adding further, the help can be even better at the spiritual level. According to him, there are many persons who serve the society much better without being known or even seen.

Since then, I am trying to follow his words of wisdom in order to help in raising the level of universal consciousness.

*****

Was It a Help

I had a friend from the Indian administrative service, whom I came in contact with in the UK, during the twelve-week training under the Colombo plan. He belonged to the Kerala cadre and hailed from Punjab. This was in the year 1990 and at that time, he was posted in Delhi on a central deputation. We had several things in common which made us close friends during the period of training, though we had not met each other before that. This friendship continued even after the training and we kept in touch with each other. I was at Kanpur at that time.

Within one year, that is, in 1991, I was also posted to Delhi on central deputation and within few months I got a residence, which was hardly two kilometres from this friend's residence. This strengthened our friendship further, and our families also came closer. We used to visit each other frequently and this continued for almost three years.

My friend's deputation to the government of India was coming to end and he was worried about it because he was not willing to go to Kerala at that point of time, mainly because of his daughter's asthma problem. So he was trying for a deputation to Punjab, which was his home state. I had a friend in the prime minister's secretariat, to whom I had also spoken for help, but somehow the proposal was not accepted. This made my friend very upset who came running to me in a very disturbed state of mind. While I was not in full agreement with his wish, still I thought of making one more effort. This time, I spoke to a junior lady colleague of mine whose father was the prime minister's principal secretary. My friend wanted an appointment with him to explain his problem. Luckily, this intervention helped and he got an appointment. Not only this, his case was then favourably considered and he got a deputation to the Punjab government for three years. This made my friend very happy and he profusely thanked me for this help. Naturally, I was also happy about it.

But our happiness was short-lived. He joined the Punjab government in the month of July 1994. Almost at the same time, I also got a posting to Kolkata on promotion and I shifted there. Our contact also became occasional. In the month of September, on a visit to Delhi, when I enquired about him from a common friend, I learnt that my friend was no more alive. He had died in an accident while driving from Chandigarh to Ludhiana, which was his home town. This was very difficult for me to bear but there was no option. I immediately rushed to Chandigarh and shared the moments of grief with his family, which gave them a lot of consolation and courage.

Quite often, I think of this incident and the question, which comes to my mind again and again, is whether it was a help or not. The message I get is that, our role in the journey of life is only to make our best efforts. The eventual outcome is the result of a large number of factors, most of which are unknown. This realisation not only keeps our ego away but also helps in accepting events as they happen.

Incidentally, the family took this development in a very positive manner and settled down in a graceful manner, in due course.

*****

One in Six Billion

Today, almost everyone feels that human values have gone down and wants the situation to change. At the same time, no one feels responsible for such a situation and hold others responsible for this. As a result, no steps are taken for the restoration of values and the situation is becoming from bad to worse. Once I had a very interesting interaction in this regard which I am sharing here.

When I was posted as principal secretary of the medical and health department of UP, I knew an officer who was trying to become the Chief Medical Officer (CMO) of a district. For this, he was making all sorts of efforts and every one knew about it. Finally, he succeeded in becoming CMO of a small district.

The very next morning, he came to my residence with a small pack of sweets (perhaps in view of the size of his district of posting). Normally, I don't meet any officials at my residence, yet I called him in my camp office. Presenting the pack of sweets, he hurriedly expressed his gratitude, though I hardly had any role in his posting. He also said that he was a victim of the system and many were responsible for his trouble. He begged for my permission to come again and narrate the details.

I was amused at this behaviour of the officer but I took it wittingly. I asked him to narrate his story then itself instead of wasting my, as well as his time by coming again. At the same time, I gave him the option of coming again but with a condition.

I asked him what the population of the world would be, to which he quickly responded by saying about 100 crores but corrected it to about 600 crores after realising that the query was about the world. Then I told him that if he wished to come some other time he should bring one person out of the six billion who would admit that he was responsible for being the cause of troubles to others. He was not at all prepared for such a response from me. His immediate reply was that it was not possible to find even one such person. I, then, told him that if there was not even one person out of the six billion who can troubles to others, then how were other people responsible for his troubles. By this time, he had understood my intension and disappeared never to be seen again.

The fact is that we are ourselves the source of our own troubles. We entertain unnecessary desires and then make compromises to attain them. If we trust the laws of Nature, even our troubles turn into blessings and opportunities. We, then, do not even think of any other person being responsible for our troubles, even if there is one or more.

*****

Blaming the Tools

During my posting at Kolkata, I used to play lawn tennis at the South Club of Kolkata. This is one of the most prestigious clubs of Kolkata, which has produced many national level players of tennis including Leander Paes. It was a real joy to play there and because of my consistency in the game, I had become quite popular among the members of the club.

I had a friend who had introduced me to the club. His son too, happened to play at the same club. He was good in the game but appeared to be somewhat too proud of himself. One day, he was playing a match with me. Being like my son, I took it easy and allowed him to win the first set with a comfortable margin. Immediately, I noticed that this win had gone to his head and instead of respecting my gesture he appeared even more proud.

Since I wanted to give him a message, I started playing seriously in the next set. He was not prepared for this and lost to me at 6-0. This upset him so much that he started checking the balls, height of the net, guts of the racket and when he found nothing wrong with them, he became sad. I approached him affectionately and told that a good player never blames the tools. The problem with him was that he lacked humility while playing and also respect for the opponent's game. While he was a good player, he underestimated his opponent and that is why he lost by a big margin. I also told him that while these qualities were necessary for a good sportsman, they were equally important for life.

The boy took my words seriously and was upset with his own behaviour. I knew he was an intelligent and smart boy with great potential and these were only minor aberrations, which needed to be corrected as soon as possible. His realisation to my suggestion pleased me too.

*****

Grace of God

Most of us have our own version of God's grace. When the events of life appear favourable to us, we feel the grace of God but when it is not so, our faith in Him is shaken and we feel that the grace of God is missing. I feel that it is not fair to blame God and by thinking this way, we show our complete ignorance about Him. The fact is that all acts of God or Nature are blessings only and they have a positive purpose behind them. Even the so-called unfavourable events fall in the category of blessings. It is a different matter that we fail to understand the purpose behind them. Quite often they happen for setting our *karmic* account and the sooner it happens, the better it is. I am sharing here, a personal incident to establish this fact.

Once, I was visiting Mirzapur in eastern UP with a good friend of mine who belonged to a political party and had been a Minister in the State Government. We both had a spiritual leaning and any interaction with him is always a joy. We travelled together in the same car from Lucknow to Mirzapur, which took about six hours. This period passed very pleasantly on account of our common interest. We reached straight to a guest house and took some rest after our lunch. We were in the same room.

In the afternoon, the attendant brought tea for us with separate milk and sugar. First, he asked my friend whether he would take sugar or not. To this, he said that he would because he had no sugar problem by the grace of God. At that time, he did not realise that I was diabetic, a fact which was very well known to him. Then the attendant turned towards me and asked the same question. I had very carefully noticed the reply of my friend and so in the same tone I said that I won't because I had sugar problem by the grace of God. This answer immediately drew the attention of my friend who realised the narrowness of his definition of God's grace. He also regretted his words, which of course was not necessary, as far as I was concerned. Then our discussion turned to the subject of God's grace and we realised the true impact of it. He fully agreed with my version which has been mentioned in the beginning.

The reason for the narrow version of God's grace is that we don't consider ourselves as a part of Nature and in the process stop following its laws. When we do so, Nature only tries to amend us and if we still don't pay heed to it, the laws of Nature operate and this operation appears to us as the lack of God's grace. Also, life can not be seen as a close- ended process, and so our sense of time may not match with the timing of Nature's process. That is why, at times, good persons appear to be suffering and not so good prospering. Once we understand this secret of Nature, we start seeing God's grace in all the events of our life.

*****

For Our Sake Only

When I was posted as principal secretary of medical and health, several programmes were being run with the help or association of international agencies. One such programme was the leprosy eradication. Once, a World Health Organisation (WHO) team visited Lucknow in connection with this programme. The head of the team was an Indian, as a result of which the communication between us became easier and the appreciation of the problem also became better. India in general and Uttar Pradesh in particular, had done a good job in this field and the leprosy rate had come down appreciably. The work was, therefore, appreciated by the visiting team.

In the evening, a dinner meeting was arranged by the department and we were interacting there. When I was conversing with the team leader at this meet, a question came to my mind as to who funds such programmes and why? Whether the funding agencies or the countries were really interested in the welfare of the poor countries or there was some other agenda also. When I put this question to the team leader, he understood my intention and gave a very realistic reply. Also, being an Indian he knew the ground realities of India well.

He said that no international funding was done only on compassionate grounds and there was always a hidden agenda, which serves the donor nation in one way or the other. In health related programmes, it was mainly to protect their own nations from those diseases, which were likely to affect those countries also. Such nations feel that as long as such diseases or health issues exist in any corner of the world, they themselves also face the danger of their onslaught. It was mainly for this reason that they funded such programmes. However, human consideration was also a factor but generally; it was subservient to the first one. This was exactly what I had in mind when I put the question to the leader and his reply confirmed my thinking.

Thereafter, I extended this fact to all acts of kindness undertaken at the individual or collective level. When we do well to others, it helps us first then the beneficiary or beneficiaries. Whether the help is in cash, kind or service, it always gives us a subtle joy, which is a great reward in itself. Greater is the selflessness in such a help, greater is the joy or reward. Going by this logic, totally selfless help gives infinite joy. Once we understand and appreciate this science of help, helping others becomes our nature, not for the sake of others but for our own sake only. Thus, from the viewpoint of return a selfless living is the most selfish way of living but such selfishness is an enlightened one or higher one.

*****

Forty Out of Forty

I have been a sharp student in my studies and mathematics was my pet subject. However, after passing High School, initially I faced some problem in this subject but the same was soon overcome and I started enjoying this subject once again. By the time half yearly examinations were conducted, I was fully prepared and confident for taking the examination.

The paper of mathematics was of forty marks and it consisted of eight questions of which six were to be solved. However, the distribution of marks to each question was little strange. Out of eight, four questions were assigned seven marks each and the remaining four were of six marks each. Thus, in order to get forty out of forty the examinee was required to solve four questions of seven marks each and any two of the remaining four questions. Thus, the choice was restricted to a great extent. Since I knew the answers of all the eight questions, I made my choice accordingly. All this, including revision was over within one and half hour while the duration of the paper was three hours and leaving the examination room before two hours was not allowed. Thus, I was to pass half an hour without doing any thing.

Suddenly, an idea came to my mind and I solved the remaining two questions also, putting a note on the top of the answer book that the examiner could check any six questions out of the eight. Not only this, I proudly shared this fact with many, feeling elated within myself. When the answer sheets were shown to us after few days, I plainly noted that I scored only thirty eight marks out of forty. On closer look, I found that the examiner had checked two questions of seven marks each and four of six marks each. Thus, the total came to only thirty-eight. This made me very upset and I immediately rushed to the teacher for complaint.

The teacher gave me a mischievous look, as if he already knew this. When I showed him my answer sheets, he admitted that all the answers were correct but said that it was only on my direction that he chose to examine any six questions. This way he had only exercised his right, which had been given by me. I almost wept on hearing this reply, but then he showed that he was happy and gave me full marks. At that time, I did not know whether he had done it out of mischief or had something else in mind.

I must have shared this incident with many and everyone was amused. But now I look at it with a different perspective. Now, I feel that it was my subtle ego, which made me solve all the eight questions and to direct the examiner to see any six. While it may be debated whether the examiner did right or wrong, the fact of my subtle ego is undebatable. My endeavour, now, is to get rid of such subtle egos which also come in the way of our good acts. Thus, I look upon at that teacher as my benefactor by his not giving me forty out of forty marks in first stance.

*****

Trials and Triumphs

The great leader of Pakistan, Begum Benazir Bhutto is now no more. Her killing has been condemned by all sensible persons throughout the world and she has been assigned the status of a martyr for her death. I have always been her admirer since I started understanding her but developed great regard for her after I saw an interview of hers on the television, sometime in September 1999. At that time, I was in Bangalore staying in a hotel. When I switched on the television, this interview was going on and it immediately caught my attention. In that interview Begum Bhutto narrated several important events of her life, which were not only interesting but also gave deep insights of her personality.

When she was narrating all such events, she said that in all great lives trials and triumphs always went together. While others generally take note of the triumphs alone, the trials part remains unknown to most of the people. She cited her own example as to how she first suffered in her father's time and then in her own family life. Amidst all these trials, she grew to a level of international status and led her country. How true her words were was amply reflected in her end subsequently.

Somehow, her phrase 'trials and triumphs' caught my attention and it still keeps coming back to me. Those who look for triumphs and more so for higher cause, have to prepare themselves for trials also. It means that there is no short cut to success. The path is always a difficult one. One has to tread it with courage and patience.

*****

Aloo Bukhara (Plum)

My first visit to the USA was in the year 1989 in the month of May. My wife accompanied me in that visit and we went to many places including New York. We thoroughly enjoyed our visit and had many good experiences. One such experience was at New York.

One day, we had our lunch in a downtown restaurant of New York. I am in a habit of eating some fruits after my meals but we found that taking a fruit in the restaurant was very expensive, more so when every dollar was important to us. We had seen many fruit sellers on the streets of New York and so decided to buy a fruit from them. As we came out of the restaurant with that intention, we saw one person selling plums. He was left with only a small quantity and so we expected a good price from him. Moreover, he was looking like an Asian.

As I and my wife were conversing in Hindi, the fruit seller was listening to us and perhaps, could also guess our nationality. When we bought two pieces of plums from him and asked for the price, he gave us a very pleasing smile. He said that there was no need of paying, as they were only neighbours. Further elaborating, he continued that he was from Pakistan while we were from India. Another reason perhaps, was the small quantity he was left with. But this was no so important for us, as was the fact of our being neighbours. We were deeply touched by his gesture and he did not accept any money even after being insisted a few times. We also took his offer with respect and gratitude. Thereafter, we exchanged some more pleasantries and parted.

This small incident comes to my mind quite often. I feel that in the name of development and progress we are forgetting to communicate with our neighbours or even our family members. This is giving rise to various conflicts and lack of true happiness. We realise this only when we are far away from them and feel lonely. This small fruit seller gave me a very pleasant lesson of life, by offering only two plums as a gift from a neighbour, whom we consider our enemy. For me, it was much more than a plum or *aloo bukhara* as we call it in Hindi.

*****

Talk to Strangers

Once I had a very strange experience during my morning walk in Vasundhara colony of Ghaziabad. This is a colony where in the development of which I took a keen interest as the housing commissioner of Uttar Pradesh. Quite often I stay there, even after I ceased to hold the job and enjoy the place. Any development in this colony still gives me joy as it relates to my memories.

During the above mentioned morning walk, I saw a school boy in his uniform on the roadside, apparently waiting for his school bus. As I approached him, I felt like talking to him in order to know about the progress of schools in the colony. With this intention, I stopped near him and asked his name very affectionately. To this, he paused for a few seconds and giving a strange look asked me as to how I was concerned with that. Certainly, I was not prepared for such a reply and was therefore, taken aback for a few seconds. I then asked him if it was this, which was taught in his school. Over this, he very innocently said, "We are taught not to talk to the strangers." This reply of his was sufficient for me to understand his dilemma and I did not raise any further question.

But this incident made me think deeply about the progress we are making. The child was not to be blamed at all because the school authorities genuinely felt that it was the best way of saving children from being cheated by strangers. However, in the process they forgot to realise that if children don't talk to strangers whom should they talk to. After all, to begin with, everyone who comes in our contact is a stranger. It is only when we meet him and talk to him that we come to know each other and the process goes on. At best, it can be advised that one should be careful and wise while interacting with a stranger but to put a blanket ban on such an interaction is certainly harmful and destructive.

All of us know that our friends were strangers to us at one point of time. Even a mother, is stranger to the child at the time of birth. It is only when they come in contact and interact that a bond is created, which is perhaps the strongest possible bond. The message therefore is that if we want to seek inner expansion we must talk to strangers and any advice contrary to this, is wrong. I wish that the modern world realised this fact, so that the joy of living is not lost.

*****

Let God Decide

Ma Anandmayee has been one of the enlightened saints of India with a large number of devotees all across the country. She was born in the erstwhile Bangladesh but spent some good time of her life in north India, particularly in Haridwar and Dehradun. She left her body in Dehradun and there is an *ashram* at that place. I had the privilege of visiting this *ashram* several times with a senior colleague of mine in service who was a close devotee of Maa. He told me many events related to Maa and this created in me a great reverence for her. I read few books also on Ma.

There is an *ashram* of Maa near Kolkata also, at a place called Golpara. I had the chance of visiting this place during my posting at Kolkata. I found the place very serene and beautiful. There we met a saint who was quite enlightened and gave us a very deep message during our conversation. He said that, most of the visitors or devotees to the temples or *ashrams* put a list of their wishes before the deity or the saint. It means that they know what is best for them and want these wishes to be fulfilled. They do not even give a chance to God to examine the list of their wishes, what to say of Him using His discretion. He further added that, the best way of seeking favours from God was to leave everything to Him and let Him decide for us. Our own role should be confined to keep on doing our best in whatever circumstances He puts us through.

This counsel was somewhat strange, even to me, at that point of time. But it made a sense to me and I contemplated over it for a long time. Thereafter, I realised that it was the most effective way of seeking the kindness of God. After all, He is the Master of the whole Universe and is capable of granting us those things, which we can not even imagine. If so why should we restrict our demands on account of our limited minds. After all, Mother Nature knows best what is most appropriate for us and therefore, it should be left on Her only.

Viewed from the opposite direction, it also means that we have to put our best while performing our duties. Nature has equipped us with so many faculties and if we do not make best use of them how can we expect Her to reciprocate in the best manner. Once this secret of Nature is understood, it is in our best interest to leave it to God to decide for us. In that case, we don't have to carry any load of desires on us. Our total energy is then deployed in doing our assigned duties.

*****

What is the Difference

1980s was a decade of my spiritual search and contemplation. During this period, I read a number of good books, came across a number of good organisations and met a number of good persons. One such occasion was visiting the Sadhu Vaswani Mission at Pune and to meet its head Dada JP Vaswani. It was in the mid-eighties and I was still learning to interact with Holy persons in a meaningful manner. The first interaction obviously used to be in the form of a greeting and in case of holy persons it was quite customary to touch their feet.

When I was to meet Dr Vaswani, I went there with the same frame of mind and touched his feet when I met him. By look and body language, *Dada* was looking very humble but I was taken aback when in response to touching his feet, he touched my feet. I was quite embarrassed at this action of his, but then he explained its significance to me. He said that as children of God or part of the same supreme soul, what was the difference between him and me. As a result, we all need to salute each other with equal reverence. This was exactly the reason why he touched the feet of those, who touched his feet.

While the explanation may look simple, it was not easy to comprehend its depth at that point of time. Even if one could comprehend it, to practice the same is very difficult. I quite often contemplate over this incident and the more I do the more reverence I develop for *Dadaji*. It also helps me in reducing the sense of duality in me, which is the cause of all our troubles. We have become so used to plurality that we either suffer with a sense of superiority or inferiority. As a result, the joy of living gets lost and we fall in a rat race to overtake others. This further creates aberration in our living and the whole life is lost without marching towards its true goal.

The message of this small incident is very great. All of us need to know our true identity and if we do so, all hierarchies in our mind will disappear. We shall then see no hierarchy in the creations of God and will duly see beautiful variety in them. The negative tendencies like superiority, inferiority, jealousy, hatred, anger, etc., then, will gradually disappear and we can live a life of perfect joy heading towards its true goal.

*****

Hen with Golden Egg

In the initial years of my service, I was posted on a sensitive post at Meerut. The job involved the regularisation or demolition of unauthorised constructions within defined limits of the city. Such constructions were in plenty and they were either being ignored or compromised by the department. There were many reasons for such a situation, including the collusion of the department at various levels. The department, known as the development authority was newly formed and was not headed properly for quite sometime. It was another valid reason for the bad state of affairs. It was at this time, that I was posted as secretary of the authority, who was the chief executive for all practical purposes.

As a young officer, I tried to streamline the working of the authority at the earliest possible. This included attending to the pending cases, which were in plenty and also to pay attention to the ongoing irregular constructions. Once, such a construction included the extension of a charitable hospital on the main road of the town. The hospital belonged to a trust owned by a known person of the town. I had come in touch with him on my previous assignment in the same district and had developed a good regard for him mainly due to his charitable activities.

Against this background, when the fact of the unauthorised construction in the hospital was attended by the authority, the owner contacted me for its disposal. I, myself, was sympathetic in the matter and wanted to settle it in the best possible manner. Since the matter was compoundable, it was decided to do the same with a sympathetic attitude. But the rules of compounding were very clear and there was only limited discretion available to me, which I used in his favour mainly on account of the purpose for which the building was being used. The owner was perhaps expecting complete waiver of the penalty, which I neither understood at that point of time, nor would have done so, even if, he would have expressed his desire. I was feeling happy that I had helped the trust in the best possible manner and the matter ended there.

Few months after the incident, I was transferred to Lucknow from Meerut. On my transfer, the head of the trust invited me over a cup of tea at his residence along with my wife. Though at a family level, we had never visited each other before, yet I accepted the invitation. While taking tea at his residence, the *Seth* called me to one corner of his house and mentioned about his hospital case. I thought he was doing so for expressing his gratitude but I was surprised when he complained of excessive penalty in the matter. I explained to him my limitations and also told that whatever help was possible had already been provided by me. But instead of being satisfied, he told me that if I needed something from him, I should have conveyed it to him. He further advised me that, while one should appear to be honest in service, some hens that could give golden eggs should always be reared.

These two sentences of the *Seth* amazed me and I had no words to say. The *Seth* whose name began with 'Shikhar' had fallen to the lowest level in my eyes. How could I explain him that honesty is a state of mind and not a show business, which I realised all through my life.

*****

One Step at a Time

Once, I was to attend a meeting in Delhi. The meeting was in the afternoon and the meeting hall was located on the fourth floor. When I reached the Ministry after obtaining the entry pass, I moved towards the lift. To my utter disappointment, I found that the lift was out of order and I was to climb up to attend the meeting. I had come to the meeting just after lunch and was not physically and mentally prepared to climb four floors. Since there was no option, I decided to climb but with reluctance and a sad state of mind.

Immediately, better sense prevailed and I thought why should I be sad in this situation. A famous quote, 'If you have not what you like, you must like what you have' came to my mind and I started seeing the situation in that perspective. I further thought that why should I think of four floors at a point of time. Instead, I started thinking of one step at one time. The whole phobia of climbing four floors then converted into a joy of taking one step at one point of time. In one step also, I thought of chanting God's name while taking a step. All this changed my state of mind completely, and I started climbing one step at a time. Soon, I was on the fourth floor to attend the meeting with cheerfulness and confidence.

This is an everyday affair with all of us. We all want to take big leaps in life in all spheres. We express our goals every now and then make no beginning. Not only so, we often blame our environment, time and others for not being able to do so. It results into continuous postponement of our action and in the process life comes to an end and it becomes too late to start. We then wait for the next life, which is so uncertain.

All those who have achieved high goals in life have wasted no time in taking the first step. Life is too short and precious to be wasted in waiting. It has been rightly said that 'even a journey of a thousand miles begins with a single step and all mighty rivers can be leapt at their source'. Once we understand the value of time and purpose of life, our confusion disappears. Life then becomes not only purposeful but a happy journey too.

In this perspective, I deeply appreciate the approach of the Dharam Bharti Mission, with whom I came in contact with recently. It says that if you want to change things for the better and achieve high goals in life then begin with yourself, begin with small and begin now. Postponement can be a costly error.

*****

The Nail Came Out

Once, I was on a visit to the University of Roorkee (now IIT) for an official work. In the morning, after my morning walk; when I was returning to the guest house, I saw a game of tennis going on in the tennis courts. Since tennis has been my favourite game, I turned towards the courts to watch the game. Incidentally, the vice chancellor and some professors who knew me well were also playing. After finishing the ongoing game, they invited me to join them. Though I was not properly dressed for the game, I accepted the offer and joined them.

Soon after the game had started, I misjudged a shot coming from the opposite side and fell on the court. The court was a cemented one and in the process my right hands fingers, as well as the thumb got badly injured. Three fingers of the hand almost fully turned backward while the nail of the thumb was badly crushed. Though medical aid was extended to me immediately but it took me months before the fingers became functional. Till now, they are not fully normal, though ten years have passed.

During the course of my recovery, I learned an important lesson. As mentioned above, the nail of my thumb was badly crushed during the fall. It used to be quiet painful but soon the natural process started replacing it with a new one. It was a slow process and the old nail was gradually being rejected. This used to irritate me and quite often I tried to remove the old nail by force. But it was a painful process and I never succeeded in it. However, this problem constantly drew my attention and I was waiting for the day when the old nail would be completely out.

It was about six months after the accident took place, when I went to an Institute at Faridabad for a lecture. During the journey also, my nail was drawing my attention. But as soon as I reached the room, I noticed that the old nail had fallen out without any pain and I felt very relieved. This process also made me think that all natural processes take their own time and there is no point in trying to expedite them. If we do so, it is a painful process.

This fact applies to all aspects of life. We often get upset over the seeming delays in our lives but there is no use of it. All problems of life get sorted out in due course and our undue concern for them is of no use. Therefore, the best way to live is to accept life as it comes. Of course, we have to do our best at every point of time.

*****

Second Class Yogi

Today, there is an ever-increasing craze for name and fame. Most of us feel that these two are the only measures to our success or greatness. Often, we adopt dubious means also, to earn name and fame. However, this is our total ignorance because our inner progress or worth has noting to do with our external name and fame. Such persons are also not able to contribute much to the society in the real sense. On the other hand, there are countless persons who have no name or fame. Yet, they are good souls and contribute to the welfare of the society withoutcreating any envy or ill will. Once this truth is realised, the craze for name and fame drops automatically and we pay greater attention to our inner development. In the process, we also grow externally and perform better in our mundane life as well.

The above lesson was learnt by me from a book on Swami Vivekanand's life. When Swami Vivekanand delivered his famous speech in the World Religion Meet at Chicago in the year 1893, he became a hero of the meet within no time. In the process, his fame spread all over the continent and many organisations started approaching him for sponsorship. For a moment, *Swamiji* got attracted to the offers for the cause of his mission but very soon he realised that the main objective of such offers was commercial and not to serve the cause of his mission. Therefore, he decided to distance himself from them.

He told his sponsors that his fame was only accidental and by no means was he a first class yogi. At best, he fell in the category of second or third class yogis. He further said that the first class yogis are never known to the world in general. They do their *sadhna* so silently that nobody comes to know of it. However, by remaining anonymous, they contribute much more to the welfare of the world. For him, the fame was an impediment. And, therefore, he would not like to ride on it. This way, he excused himself and went on further in a natural manner to pursue his mission.

Here lies the secret of *Swamiji's* success. He lived only nine years after his famous speech, but during this short period he revolutionised religion. It transformed from passive dogmas to dynamic ways of living for the welfare of human society. The message is that we grow best when we work selflessly without any craze for name and fame. It is a different matter, if we get them too in due course. Our society has many such silent workers. They may not be well-known but they make a difference to things and people around them.

*****

Land for Grave

I have a young Muslim friend who is in his thirties. He is a very enthusiastic person and always carries a cheerful disposition. He is also a member of the Kabir Peace Mission and often visits me. One day, when he came to me, he appeared even more cheerful. On being asked about the reason, he told me that he was happy because he had purchased the land for his grave on the previous day. This was something for which I was neither prepared nor had heard of before. I knew that Muslims bury the dead body in the earth but the fact that, for this, land has to be arranged in advance was a surprise to me. Hearing the cause of his cheerfulness, I became curious and desired to know more about the deal.

He told me that land in Lucknow was getting costlier day by day and the same was the case with graveyards also. He was happy because he could get the land at a reasonable rate and he could pay the price easily. He further said that arranging land for the grave was an essential responsibility and he could get rid of it so early. Now onwards, he would be able to live peacefully. All this amazed me and I wondered at his preparedness for death at such an early age.

Then I enquired about the measurement of the land he had purchased for his grave. He told me the graveyard he had chosen was a prestigious one and only six feet by two and a half feet land is given to the buyer. In this way, he had purchased only fifteen square feet of land, as more than that was not available to anyone. He was quite satisfied with that also.

His narration of these facts increased my respect for him. But more than that, it was the message he gave to all living persons which is important. Who does not know the fact that life is a journey from the womb to the tomb? But how many take it that way? Most of us spend our lives in accumulating wealth and other material possessions. Quite often these possessions are acquired at the cost of others. While excessive possessions are a potential cause of sorrow for the possessor also, this tendency also deprives many others of their essential needs. In this way, the resources of the nation are wasted. The fact that at the end of this journey only six feet by two and half feet land will be available to us should be enough reason for us to live gracefully, as well as to let others live gracefully. My young friend demonstrated this point so simply and easily by purchasing the land for his grave.

*****

Metamorphosis

I had a friend who was a doctor in the Sanjay Gandhi Post Graduate Institute of Medical Sciences, Lucknow who was a senior professor in the department of gastro- enterology. His wife was also a senior professor in another department. Both husband and wife were known for their competence and patient care. It was always a joy to interact with them and I always enjoyed their company.

This doctor friend of mine was suddenly detected for a stomach ailment, which called for immediate opening of his stomach. When the surgeon did so, they found that the patient was suffering with cancer of intestines, which was in an advance stage. Everyone was surprised as well as shocked to see this and more so in case of the patient himself being a gastro-enterologist. Seeing the condition of the stomach, it was guessed that the patient would not live for more than six months.

One can imagine the state of mind of the patient in such a position. But this friend of mine was a different person. Not only was he different, his family members also were different. All of them refused to say 'no' to life and accepted the reality with grace. The doctor patient had risen in his life with a humble background and gave to the society much more than he had taken from it. Even in such a condition, he decided to give the society whatever he could during the expected short span of life.

He made a request to the director of the institute and asked for the services of a stenographer. He wanted to dictate the history of his life and through that biography he wished to pass on all the wisdom he had acquired in his short life. The request was considered and accordingly, he started dictating. Not only this, he continued to deliver lectures also, as long as he was in a position to do so. All along his condition was deteriorating, though at slower pace than was predicted. He and his family had also to entertain a good number of relatives and well-wishers who came to see them, as they learnt about the development.

I also visited my friend few times during this period. His actual condition was never reflected on his face and his responses were always positive. He was continuing with his book, afraid only of the deadline set to his life, but he was confident of seeing it through. Eventually, he won and his book was released fifteen days before he passed away eternally. The book was released by the then governor of UP. It was one of the most solemn events of my life. There was not a single eye without tears. The author had challenged Nature and had lived a full year against an optimistic lease of six months.

The Book was titled as *'Metamorphosis'*, an apt description of the author's life and a true inspiration for others.

*****

Artificial Gold

We have a known family, which lives in the same locality in Lucknow in which we live. At present, only the husband and wife stay at Lucknow as their children have settled outside. Often, they visit us and at times his wife also visits alone.

During one such visit, his wife came to my house alone during the day. It was during my office hours and my wife also, was alone at home. That day an incident took place in which the gold chain of the lady was snatched by a thief, when she was near my home. The lady was frightened by this incident and took shelter in my house narrating the whole development. Her husband being out of town, she could not even think of reporting the incident to the police.

Next day, when her husband returned I advised him to report the matter to the police, which he did immediately. I also spoke to the inspector general of police, who happened to be a good friend of mine, apart from being a good and efficient police officer. The main purpose of my speaking to him was to convey to him the perception of law and order situation in the town, which is greatly damaged by such incidents. As far as this particular case was concerned, I expected no relief.

But to my utter surprise, the relief came very soon. Within three days, my friend got a call from the police station that some chains were recovered from a gang and they could visit the police station to identify theirs. The couple did so promptly and picked up a chain, which they claimed to be theirs. The chain was restored to them immediately. This was a great surprise for all of us and the lady's joy knew no bounds.

The next day, the lady was advised to consult the goldsmith about the genuineness of the gold. When they went their, to their utter dismay it turned out to be of artificial gold. Their entire joy disappeared in no time and now they were sadder than they were, at the time of loss. The matter was again reported to the Inspector General who helped in recovering the real one.

Without going into the intricacies of the matter, I looked upon this incident with some amusement also. The lady, herself, being incapable of distinguishing between real and artificial gold, enjoyed both equally and in this particular case, she enjoyed the artificial gold even more than the real gold. But the same artificial gold gave her so much sorrow, when identified by the gold smith.

The message is that, most of us keep on enjoying artificial things and waste life in the process. Only when we come to know of the reality, the joy disappears and we try to seek real joy, which is within all of us. Let us, therefore, give up, our artificial joy of objects and seek the real one of divinity.

*****

Malaysian Driver

Once, I was on a visit of Malaysia along with my wife. The visit was in connection with a conference on security and the venue was Penang. It is a beautiful island and a popular tourist destination. We thoroughly enjoyed our visit and went around the whole island.

During the course of our stay at Penang, one day I hired a taxi for going around the town for half a day from 9 a.m. to 1 p.m. for the two of us. The charges were fixed at 120 ringgits. This arrangement was made on the previous evening. During the dinner when we shared this information with some of the other participants, two of them got interested in joining us. We had no objection in that because it would have given us company as well as we would have saved some ringgits also. When contacted, the taxi driver also had no objection but now demanded 160 ringgits for all the four. We all agreed to this arrangement.

Next morning, the taxi arrived at the hotel five minutes before 9 a.m. and the driver informed me about his arrival. At that time, we were on the breakfast table along with the other two participants who were to join us on the trip. Somehow, we noticed that they were reluctant to join us. My guess was that they changed the idea during the night, perhaps on account of the cost involved but were not very forthright about it. Instead of conveying their doubts, they started advising us also to drop the trip. Since no advance had been paid, they also suggested that the driver be made to wait without conveying our decision. For sometime, we tried to convince them about the economy of the trip as well as the embarrassment that would be caused in the process, but failed. We then decided to go ourselves, even if it meant paying 160 ringgits.

As a result, when I and my wife approached the waiting taxi it was close to 10 a.m. When we told the driver about the difficulty of the other two passengers, he smilingly accepted the situation and agreed to take us on the previous arrangement of 120 ringgits only. This came as a surprise to us, and which only raised our respect for him.

The driver took us around the tour in a very cordial way and showed no hurry in order to compensate the delay. Not only this, he worked as our guide also and took us around to many places, which we had not thought of. He also helped us in our shopping as well as in taking food, which took more time than what we had planned for. All this resulted in delay and when we returned to the hotel, it was 2:30 p.m. It meant that we had delayed him by one and half hour.

I, naturally, felt like paying him more than the agreed amount and offered some extra ringgits. But I was amazed to see his response. He very firmly and politely turned down the offer. Instead, he asked whether we were satisfied with his services, which we obviously were more than our expectations. Though I could not pay him more money, but I certainly gave him a silent salute and also saw a glimpse of nation building in his gesture.

*****

Pet on the Road

Once, I was staying with a nephew of mine at New Jersey in USA. I used to get up early there also, and go for a morning walk. The place around was very clean and scenic but there used to be hardly any person on the road. Even if there were any, there was hardly any exchange of words except a greeting by wavering of the hand and that too, from a distance.

One day, during such a morning walk I saw a lady with her small pet on the other side of the road. As usual, I greeted her by waving my hand. To this, her response was different and she responded by uttering some nice words. Somehow, I felt that she was keen to talk to me and since I also find such conversations very educative, I also made the same gesture and we started walking together.

Soon, I noticed that she was interested in India because her father had been an army officer during the British rule. As a result, she had spent few years of her childhood in India. Perhaps, that was the reason why she showed interest in me, as she had guessed me to be an Indian. Anyway, we exchanged many things about India and British life and overall, it was a very good exchange.

While we were walking on the footpath, she noticed that her pet was about to attend to Nature's call. I also noticed the same and was keen to see how she would handle the situation. But I was pleasantly surprised to note that she had came prepared for the same and immediately took out a polythene bag from her pocket and took the excreta of her pet in that bag. This was her reflex action without being conscious of my presence. Then she wrapped the polythene bag and put it in a paper bag and kept back in her pocket. As she finished all this, she was back in the conversation with me.

I was amazed to notice all this and conveyed my feelings to her. It was a surprise to her that in India people take out their pets only to use roads and pathways as toilets for them. What a difference between the two cultures. While we may boast of our ancient culture and spiritual heritage, we fail badly in displaying modern culture and civic sense in our day- to- day living. This is the reason why our ancient values are losing their meaning and in the process life is becoming difficult.

Who says we have nothing to learn from the West? Culture is not a monopoly of one country or race. Each Society has a culture of its own and in modern times when the world is becoming smaller and smaller in terms of communication and reach; we must take the best from every society. Then only our scripture's message of 'Vasudhaiva Kutumbkam' will have any meaning. Otherwise, it will remain just a scriptural phrase.

*****

NCC Camp

In the year 1965, I attended a National Cadet Corps (NCC) camp for about fifteen days. At that time, I was in the first year of my graduation. My elder brother was also in the same college studying in the second year of graduation. We both were supposed to attend that camp. Since the camp was to be held just before *deepawali* festival, it meant being away from home during the festival, which certainly did not make the occasion very welcoming.

In view of this, many students applied for exemption including my elder brother. The exemption was sought mainly on medical grounds, which required a fake medical certificate. It was not difficult to get one even during those times. My elder brother also resorted to the same practice and managed to get exemption. The idea of seeking exemption did not even occur to me and doing so on the basis of a false medical certificate was even more remote to me. As a result, I had to attend the camp, though I too was not very happy about it for reasons mentioned above.

This was my first experience of collective living and that too, in somewhat uncomfortable conditions. Waking up early in the cold season (at that time *deepawali* days used to be quite cold and more so in the open ground), taking bath in cold water, strict adherence to meal timings as well as the quantity, the poor quality of food, etc., were the factors which always gave a regretful feeling. At that time, the imagination of the comfort of those, who had sought exemption on one ground or the other used to add salt to the injury. But there was no option but to undergo all the drill. Not only this, the behaviour of our friends occupying some rank in the NCC was even worse than the real officers.

Somehow, the days passed and we started enjoying the so-called suffering. Many aspects of such a life were new to us, which we would have missed, had we not attended the camp. Gradually, the envy with those who had sought exemption started disappearing with a feeling of being fortunate replacing it. Though we were given an option to spend the day with our families, the evening celebration was in the camp only. The fun during that celebration is still a memorable event. Overall, this camp gave me a good lesson of life, which helped a lot in leading a successful one.

It has been rightly said that there is no elevator to success; the path is through the staircase. The heights achieved through the elevator are equally short-lived. The NCC camp taught me this secret very convincingly.

*****

Anil Ambani's Lunch

Mr Anil Ambani used to be a member of the UP development council during a particular regime. This was the highest body responsible for taking important development decisions in the state. Many well-known persons in the field of industry, banking, media and commerce were members of this body. The council used to meet at various places and senior officers of various development departments were also invited to attend these meetings.

In one such meeting held in Delhi, I was also present as a special invitee. At that time, I was posted as principal secretary of the medical and health department. The meeting was held in Ashoka hotel and went very well. After the meeting, we all were invited to join the buffet lunch, which was arranged quite lavishly.

I normally take a light lunch but the menu being quite rich, I had no option but to take what was served by the hotel. Soon after I started eating my lunch sitting on a side table, I noticed Anil Ambani also coming to the same table and occupying a seat. He had not taken his lunch but immediately, a battery of bearers along with their boss approached him to seek orders. To this, his response was very interesting. He refused to accept any item already served. Instead, he ordered for two pieces of *idly* along with little *sambhar*. Of course, it was promptly served to him and that was all he took for lunch.

While his simple lunch created some envy in me as I had missed this opportunity, it also made me contemplate over the matter. Most of us feel that the goal of life is to increase our consumption level and we feel envious of those who are wealthy. But wealth does not necessarily mean that our consumption will go up. Our basic needs remain the same and if they are comfortably met, that should be enough reason for our happiness. Any acquisition beyond need becomes a burden if it is not shared with others or utilised for a higher cause. All those who acquire wealth, position, fame, etc., can remain happy only when they use such acquisitions for others.

It is more true in case of food. Hazrat Mohammad Sahab used to say that food should be taken only when one is very hungry and only half stomach should be filled. If one does no, he will always be healthy. A well-known naturopath of India says the same thing in other words. According to him, half the food we take keeps us alive and the other half keeps the doctors alive. If one follows this advice, he himself remains happy and lets others also be happy.

Anil Ambani's lunch proved this fact amply and also revealed the secret of his good health and mind.

*****

Inner Management

Once I was travelling from Delhi to Lucknow by Lucknow Mail. I had a booking in the AC first class coach and my berth was the lower berth. On the opposite lower berth, there was another gentleman whom I did not recognise. Both the upper berths were vacant to begin with, but just before the train started moving, two gentlemen entered the cabin, kept their briefcases on the upper berths and soon left the cabin. This created an impression that both of them were unauthorised passengers and did not have any reservations. However, I didn't take any notice of it but the other passenger was certainly not happy about it. Since both left the cabin almost immediately, he could say nothing to them.

Early in the morning, I heard some harsh exchange of words in the cabin. It so happened that both the upper berth passengers returned to the cabin in the early hours and put on the light. This disturbed my co-passenger and he objected to it, somewhat angrily. This was not liked by the other two passengers and they too responded in the same tone. On this, my co-passenger termed them as unauthorised travelling with the connivance of the railway staff. This was too much for them and all this resulted in a heated exchange of words. By this time, I was fully awake and wanted to understand the situation. Firstly, I tried to calm them down with a firm and polite request. Somehow, they responded to my request and all of us started to discuss the matter. As a result, the following facts came out.

The two passengers who had occupied the upper two berths were railway officers occupying the post of executive and superintendent engineers. They were on their official duty and were to conduct certain studies on the moving train in the engine. That is why they had left the cabin just after keeping their brief cases. After completing the study, they came back to the cabin in the early hours and were quite tired. Since it was the winter season, the cold had added to their fatigue. So, they were in a hurry to take some rest and in the process disturbed my co-passenger. After knowing all these facts, both sides realised their hasty response and felt sorry about it.

The surprising fact was that my co-passenger was the director of a reputed management institute of Lucknow. I knew him by name and had talked over the phone several times, but had never met him. The acquaintance made him feel guilty also, but I tried to convince him that such mistakes were normal and one only needs to learn lessons from such incidents for the future. Incidentally, the train was quite late and this provided us an opportunity to know each other more closely and when we left the Lucknow railway station, there was a tough competition between the two sides for realising their mistakes.

I told my co-passenger that it was a problem of 'inner management' which is perhaps more important than 'outer management' taught by him all through his life.

*****

Both Disappointed

*O*nce I came across an industrialist cum businessman along with his only son in the *ashram* of my spiritual master Swami Bhoomananda Tirtha at New Delhi. At that time, I was posted as the regional development commissioner for Iron and Steel. With me was also a friend of mine from Kanpur. He knew the industrialist because he had some industry in Kanpur also. My friend was quite surprised to see the industrialist in the *ashram*, as he was supposed to be a very materialistic person. When enquired, it was revealed that his only son had become a recluse and took no interest in his business. It was only on his son's insistence that he had come to the *ashram*. While the purpose of his son was to seek spiritual guidance, the father had come to seek *Swamiji's* blessing for bringing back his son to business.

When my friend introduced me to the businessman and told my designation, he got keenly interested in me and sought an appointment in my office. From my side, I thought that his son's detachment with the world must have had a deep impact on the father and perhaps he would discuss with me only this matter. At that time, I was a beginner in the field of spirituality and didn't understand human nature very deeply. I thought if the businessman also turned spiritual, it would be a greater benefit to the society. Considering all these points, I fixed up an appointment with him in my office only a few days after.

The gentleman came to my office on the appointed day. When I started the discussion about his son, he appeared disinterested and even my repeated references made no impact on him. On this, I thought that he must be very sad about it and, therefore, avoided the discussion. But soon, he came to his point. At that time, steel was a controlled commodity and had a premium on it. This gentleman wanted some quota of steel so that he could earn some money by selling it in the black market. Firstly, I didn't believe it but I found that he was quite serious about it. Not only this, he openly offered some share to me also.

I was dumbfounded by his offer. There were no words with me to respond. I had genuinely expected him to talk something sensible, particularly in the back drop of his only son's renunciation. But everyone is not fortunate to rise above the world and this gentleman was one of them. For him, money was everything and its accumulation was the only purpose of his life. Perhaps, that was the reason why his son had developed a disliking for the material world. But there was no point in talking to him about all this. Therefore, I begged him to excuse me and our meeting ended abruptly.

In a way, this appointment was a disappointment for both of us.

*****

Refusal by Coolie

Once I was waiting at the Aligarh railway station to board a train for Punjab. The train was to leave at about 8:30 p.m. but it was getting delayed. I had a coolie for my luggage who was also waiting with me. I was carrying my packed food for dinner. Seeing the train getting late, I ate the food on the platform only sitting on a bench. After food, I bought two oranges one for myself and the other for the coolie waiting with me. While doing so, I was filled with compassion and with that subtle ego within; I offered one orange to the coolie. The coolie was absorbed in his own world and perhaps this offer disturbed his absorption. As a result, he declined my offer saying that he was in no mood to eat at that time.

For a moment, I felt hurt and also insulted. It took me sometime to come to terms with this small incident. At that time, I was reading a book of Vivekananda, in which it is often mentioned that it is we, who need the world and not vice versa. Whenever someone offered his or her service for the society, the first advice he gave to others was to drop the ego while serving others. Since this advice of his was fresh in my mind, I immediately related this incident with his advice. It, then, became clear to me that it was my subtle ego of giving, which hurt me and not his refusal.

That was the early period of my service. Fortunately, certain incidents of this period turned me into a spiritual seeker. At that time, I was in the initial stages of seeking and such incidents were certainly programmed by Nature as practical demonstrations of what I was reading in the books. The refusal by the coolie was one of them. Since then my perception about giving to others, in whatever form, changed completely and I started taking all such opportunities as grace of God.

In due course, I also realised that when we give with the right attitude to the right person, we receive much more from Nature. The return may not come from the same person or persons, but it comes from sources, which are often unknown to us. Therefore, to live a life based on calculations or expectations proves counter productive and mars the joy of giving. Our concern should only be our joy in giving and once it becomes our nature then our returns are taken care of by Nature itself. In that case, even the joy of receiving multiplies. The simple refusal of the orange by the beggar taught me this lesson for life.

*****

The Coffee Machine

In the year 1989, I travelled to USA via Japan. My wife was also with me. The first leg of our journey was from Delhi to Tokyo where we stayed for three days. The next journey was from Tokyo to San Francisco on the western side of USA. While travelling on this route, one gains time, which is quite an interesting experience. For example, if we leave Tokyo in the evening of Sunday, the arrival at San Francisco would be in the morning of Sunday. Thus, one can enjoy two Sunday's in the same week. This was to happen with us also, as we were scheduled to leave Tokyo on a Sunday evening.

While we were waiting at the Tokyo airport, the flight got delayed by about an hour. During this waiting period, I felt like taking a cup of coffee. In my pocket, there were some yens as I had converted most of the yens into dollars before leaving Japan. When I went to a coffee stall and read the price of a cup of coffee, my possession felt short by few yens. At that time, one yen was equal to about ten paise in India. I thought that the vendor would oblige me by accepting few yens less and give a cup of coffee.

With this in mind, I approached the salesgirl, who could understand a bit of English. I tried to explain my problem to her and she could understand also. While she wanted to help me, she expressed her inability to do so because the machine could not operate even if the amount was one yen less than the exact price. At that moment, I remembered the vendors of my own country, where the relationship between the seller and buyer existed on direct basis and not through the machine. As a result, they can use their discretion in such matters.

The idea behind narrating this small incident is not to condemn mechanisation, but to show how this large-scale mechanisation has taken away the joy of human relationships. The world today is growing very fast but with this change, human relationships are also changing. In this process, it is difficult to say whether happiness is also increasing. Why difficult, it is certain that the happiness index of mankind has come down with the so-called development. It raises questions about where we are going wrong.

We are going wrong in the sense that in the modern age man itself has been reduced to a machine. He has been made to believe in certain norms of life, which dub him as modern and successful. Thus, success has been the sole goal of life. Whether it is accompanied by peace or not is not important. The whole turmoil of the modern world is on account of this madness. If we pause for a moment and analyse our life, there is every likelihood of finding a way to happiness. But most of us are too busy to do so and in the process miss the essence of life, which is joy and happiness.

Let us not lose the human connection, as we modernise ourselves. This is the main agenda before us in modern times. For this, we have to be our own masters and not slaves to machines.

*****

Secret of Economic Growth

Once I was on an election commission's duty as an observer in the state of Bihar. It was for assembly election in the year 1995. Bihar in itself is a poor state, but the Araria district, the area where I was assigned duty was even poorer. At that time, I was posted at Kolkata and there was a direct train from Sealdah to the place of my duty.

In my very first visit to the place, I was amazed to see the socio-economic condition of the place. People there, were simple and poor but their happiness index was certainly higher than their urban or more prosperous counterparts. This trait of theirs was exploited fully by their leaders, who saw their vested interest in keeping them in that condition only. Overall, it was a very rich experience, which not only increased my sensitivity towards poor people but also revealed to me the secret of economic growth.

One day, while travelling on a countryside road in the district, I started conducting a survey of people walking or cycling on the road side. The two parameters, I had in mind were their clothes and footwear's. I observed both these possessions carefully. As far as clothing was concerned, I noticed that half of them wore only an undergarment (*baniyan*) and in good number of cases it was a torn one. There were some who were bare- bodied, some with damaged *kurta* and only about one in ten had put on a shirt or *kurta* in good condition. More or less, same was the situation with women, many of whom wrapped their upper parts with a *sari* worn by them. In the case of footwear, half of them were barefoot and most of the remaining wore a cheap rubber *chappal*, damaged in good number of cases. Only about one out of ten had proper shoes on their feet.

I was touched to see this condition of the majority of people. My attention went to the wardrobes of those rich people who have countless clothes and shoes only to remain unutilised while depriving others. I was not a student of economics but by common sense thought that this could not be the way of economic development. Certainly, it would be much faster, if the entire population had access to their minimum needs. If each Indian woman was to possess one pair of *sari*, man one pair of shirt and all of them one pair of footwear, the textile and footwear industry would grow at a much faster rate than it does now. The same is true for other needs.

Economists and planners have failed to bring equity in the development process. I feel that all the disorders of the society are mainly on account of the increasing gap between the rich and the poor. Such growth models can not sustain for a long time and today's recession has lot to do with this failure. Gandhiji had this model of growth in mind which, we failed to follow, and are paying the price for it. Let us review our priorities and learn from our mistakes.

After the above visit, I also started possessing only one pair of shoes and few sets of clothes. Surely, I have been a happier person since then.

*****

No Change in Medicine

This incident relates to the year 1983. I was then posted as district collector of Basti in UP. Basti was a big district at that time and also a very backward one. Floods used to be the annual feature of the area and villagers were quite accustomed to the allied problems. However, the district administration used to take all the necessary steps to minimise the difficulties of the people. As collector of the district, I also tried my best to do so.

During the floods of 1983, I was once on a tour of a remote area of the district. I had left the headquarters early in the morning and it was late noon when I was returning back. On the way, I felt very tired and also feverish. Therefore, I asked my driver to stop at some dispensary on the way so that I could take some medicines. Soon he stopped at a government Primary Health Centre (PHC). The doctor was present there and gave me some medicines. The medicines were loose tablets, which he gave me from a bottle. There was only one tablet, which he prescribed to me to be taken three times a day and hoped that I would be all right within three days. Accordingly, he gave me the necessary quantity. I took the first dose there itself. On enquiry, the doctor also told me that my problem was quite common in that season and the medicines given to me were quite effective.

When I reached the district headquarter, the Chief Medical Officer (CMO) of the district also came to know of my indisposition. Soon he came to see me and brought with him a packet of medicines which were not only many in number but also costly. When I enquired from him, whether these medicines were also available to general patients, he replied in the negative and added that they were specially procured for me from the market. He also emphasised that I must take those medicines, if I wanted to be normal soon.

My attention, then, went to the words of the doctor at PHC who had told me that the medicines given by him were quite effective in common people. With that in mind, I politely asked the CMO to let me try the common man's medicines. One additional reason for doing so was the simplicity of the dosage, which was very complex in case of the medicines brought by the CMO. Though not convinced he had no option and left along with the medicines.

I took the simple medicines for three days and became quite normal as per the hopes of the doctor at PHC. At this, I felt very happy and shared this experience with many. I also felt jealous of a common man who gets cured with simple medicines while an important person has to take complicated and expensive treatment for the same disease.

*****

Honour of the Back Seat

I started living in my own house at Lucknow in the year 1996. Only few days later, I met one retired gentleman living in the same locality. He was a Lt. General in the Indian army and had retired from the post of vice-chief. I had heard of his simplicity from others but meeting him was a very pleasant experience. His house was a moderate one but maintained very meticulously with lot of greenery inside, as well as outside. In fact, our first meeting was at a time when he was taking care of the greenery maintained by him outside his house along the road. This scene left a deep mark on me and we gradually became very close to each other.

In due course, I also learnt about the important positions he had occupied in the Indian army. Not only this, he came from a very good background with many friends and relatives in important positions. Against the background of these facts, his simplicity assumed even greater meaning. In the process, my regard for him only grew with time. He also became a life member of the Kabir Peace Mission and contributed a lot in its activities.

Once, this gentleman was invited to an important function of the mission. We had earmarked a prominent seat for him in the front row but our guest was nowhere to be seen, though he had promised to come. Suddenly, he was spotted sitting in the back row and could be brought to the front row only after great persuasion. For him, sitting at the back appeared to be quite normal and there was no gimmick behind it. Later also, such situations arose several times.

This set me thinking about those who occupy or try to occupy the front seats, in whatsoever field they are, fully knowing their place. Such persons at times have to be reminded their place and when this is done, they feel insulted and may even become our enemies. A wise or great person never does so. On the other hand, they feel more comfortable in giving the front place to others. In this way, they make themselves more honourable than those occupying the front seats. At the same time, they pre-empt any chance of being insulted or made to feel small.

The gentleman being mentioned above is one of them. Everytime, when he does so, he goes up in my esteem. The name of the gentleman is Lt. General Vijay Singh and even after crossing 75 years, he is healthy and happy. One of the secrets of this is the honour he gives to the back seat.

*****

Joy of Ignorance

Life is a cycle of joys and sorrows. Most of us are carried away by them and feel happy or unhappy accordingly. Our seers have contemplated a lot on this subject and have advised us to rise above both of them. They say that there is no absoluteness about them and both are fleeting moments of life. In other words, joy and sorrow are only external happenings and affect us only when we come to know of such happenings. If we are ignorant about them, they create no effect on us. Also, the same event creates a different feeling in different persons. It depends upon our relationship with the event at that point of time. Had they been absolute, they would create same feelings in all of us and even when we didn't know about them. In addition, the impact of any event, good or bad, fades with time and we remain affected neither by a good event nor by a bad event in due course of time.

I narrate a personal experience to support the above. It was in May 1983 when I was posted as district magistrate in Basti. At that time, one of my close friends was posted as district magistrate in Almora (at that time Uttarakhand was a part of UP). He invited us to visit Almora, which is one of the most beautiful hill stations. Those days, my father-in-law who was in Delhi was not well and there was a risk to his life. However, after being assured that there was no immediate danger, I decided to undertake the trip with my family. My friend had made good arrangement for our stay and travel within his district.

There were several places worth visiting including Ranikhet known as the 'Queen of Hills'. Overall, we enjoyed our stay and had nice time.

At that time, communication by telephone was not very advanced. Hill districts, in particular, had poor services and it was very difficult to get in touch even with Delhi. As a result, we had no communication about the condition of my father-in-law. As we were returning to Basti from Almora, we stopped briefly at Lucknow, and I contacted Delhi from there. I learnt that my father-in-law had passed away two days back and by that time he had been cremated also. This came to us as a great shock and I, with my wife travelled to Delhi, the same evening and observed the mourning period there.

While all this was being done, the philosophical thoughts about our joy at Almora and sorrow after learning about the death kept occupying my mind. This contemplation made me believe that our joy is nothing but our ignorance and by the same logic our sorrow is equally our ignorance. A wise person neither gets elated with joy nor gets depressed by sorrow. Since then, I am trying to imbibe this wisdom in me.

*****

Went Without Dinner

*M*any times, I travel from my hometown Muzaffarnagar to Lucknow by Nauchandi Express. This train runs between Saharanpur to Allahabad and is very convenient at least for the above journey. Leaving at about 6:15 p.m., it reaches Lucknow early in the morning. Thus, it is quite efficient in terms of the time taken. It has no AC first class compartment and also no pantry car. I, therefore, carry my simple packed dinner and eat it at the next stop in Meerut, where it stops for about half an hour. I also don't bother any official of my department at Meerut mainly because I don't want to be disturbed by them.

During one such journey, I had just finished my packed food when a senior officer of a particular department boarded the train at Meerut and occupied a berth just opposite to mine. Being head of his department, a large number of local officers along with many officials had come to see him off. They all were trying to appease him and had brought a lavish dinner packed for him from a good restaurant of the town. Since the officer knew me and my position, he was feeling somewhat embarrassed also, particularly when there was none to take care of me. However, I was amusedly watching all this and enjoying my reading, which is my main occupation during such journeys.

As soon as the train left the Meerut station, the officer started settling down. First of all, he arranged his dinner packets properly and while doing so offered me his food, which was obviously in plenty. Since I had already finished my dinner, I politely declined the offer and got engrossed in my reading. After few minutes, he got ready to take his food and started opening his packets. I noticed that as he opened one pack, he immediately closed it and kept aside. He did the same with other packs also and eventually, kept all the packets beneath his berth.

This created some anxiety in me and I enquired from him as to what went wrong with the food. He hesitatingly told me that all the packets contained non-vegetarian food and since it was a Tuesday, it was of no use to him. The poor fellow, therefore, had to go without dinner. May be he took some snacks at the next stop of the train.

This incident has a message in it. Firstly, simple requirements should not be made complicated. Secondly, there should be proper communication in case of personal requirements more so, when they are made by those who don't know you closely. Thirdly, too much expectation from your subordinates quite often becomes troublesome. I don't know whether the gentleman travelling with me learnt any of these or not, I certainly got reinforced in my decision of carrying packed food and not bothering my subordinates unnecessarily.

*****

A Stitch in Time

The study of the lives of many great men and women of the world reveal that they were great not because they occupied high positions, had more riches or earned fame. Their greatness lied in the manner in which they attended to small matters. I am fortunate in the sense that I have studied many biographies and autobiographies of such people, and learnt many useful things from them. The three great persons who have influenced me most are Kabir, Swami Vivekananda and Mahatma Gandhi. Each of them had their own greatness but one quality, which is common in all great persons, is their simplicity. However, all are not able to appreciate the joy of those who lead a simple life.

I have been trying to imbibe this quality in me since I came in touch with these great persons through books. I am fully convinced that the main secret of our happiness is our simplicity. Lesser are our needs; greater is the measure of our joy. I also believe that lesser needs need not necessarily mean deprivation in any respect. On the other hand, such life is self-preserving and mutually beneficial. When we consume only as per our need, others get their share in a natural manner, creating greater happiness all around. My experience is that there is always a scope of reducing our need without any compromise with comfort or happiness. I am going to support this by a very simple event of my life.

In April 2008, I was to go on a personal visit to Dubai for about five days. When I was preparing for the visit, I noticed that my bathroom *chappals* were not in a very good condition and it appeared risky to carry them for the trip. Since I keep only one pair of *chappals*, the only alternative was to buy a new pair. As I was going to act on this, a thought came to my mind that why should I not get my *chappals* stitched to avoid any risk of it breaking. I then did the same thing and by spending only a rupee or two, my fear was gone. The *chappals* gave me no problem during the visit and I felt quite happy about my decision. The *chappals* then lasted for more than one year without any problem.

This is just one example of the extent of simplicity one can go for. It is only a question of paying little attention to little things. But today's world is so materialistic that such issues have no priority for most of us and we acquire material things without assessing their needs. In the process, we not only deprive others of their needs but also add to our own worries. No wonder, the happiness level is going down with the rise in income levels.

As a student, I had read a proverb that said, 'a stitch in time saves nine'. For me, it became literally true. One timely stitch of my *chappal* saved my ninety rupees at least for one year.

*****

People Honour the Honour

It is perhaps the law of Nature that we all salute to the rising Sun and not the setting Sun. Similarly, when we get sudden success, fame, recognition or riches, people rush to us irrespective of the fact whether it was well-deserved or not. Many times, even those persons hang around us, who have had no liking for us. At times, this may annoy us also but there is no point in getting annoyed and the whole process should be accepted with equanimity, more so when such an achievement is well-deserved. While it is easy to say so, in actual life it may be difficult to follow. An incident of Ravindra Nath Tagore's life may be of help in appreciating this point and consequently in following.

When Tagore was conferred with the Nobel Prize in literature for his work *'Gitanjali'* (1912) in the year 1913, it gave a big surprise to the literary circle of Calcutta. Obviously, it was so for Tagore also, as often is the case with such recognition. But the case of Tagore was somewhat different. Tagore was never given the due recognition at home and his contemporaries in the literary circle never thought so highly of him. One reason for this could be their silent jealousy against Tagore on various counts. Tagore also knew this but remained aloof as long as it didn't affect him.

The news of the Nobel Prize to Tagore intensified this jealousy even more but that was a fact. Tagore had shifted to Shantiniketan by that time near Bolpur. A big group of the literary circle of Calcutta, therefore, decided to proceed to Shantiniketan to honour Tagore and the same was communicated to him. Tagore knew that most of the people who were coming to honour him had no great regard for him and they were coming only because he had been conferred with the Nobel Prize. So he was not very happy about it and shared his feeling with some close friends of his at Shantiniketan. His words were that the delegation was coming not to honour him but to honour his honour. The friends also knew the fact and understood Tagore's dilemma. However, one of the friends advised Tagore to remain as gracious as he had always been and receive the delegation. Tagore conceded to this advice and the event went off gracefully. Perhaps, Tagore would have done so on his own accord also.

The message of this small narrative is that one should take 'success' and 'failure' with equanimity. If one does not feel much elated in the former, the latter also will not have an adverse effect. Tagore had several tragedies in life but he was equally calm in those periods. That is why in due course, he not only won the true respect of his colleagues but of the whole world. But this does not happen in one day and one has to strive for it the whole life.

*****

How Much Do We Need

*M*any years back, I was staying in a forest rest house at Kanpur. In this forest, there was a long track where some people used to come there for their morning walks. The track is narrow, zigzag and runs into few kilometres. Overall, it is a great joy to be in the lap of Nature and enjoy its ambience while walking. During my stay, a friend of mine joined me for the morning walk and we both were walking on that narrow path. It was difficult to walk together and therefore, I was walking behind him and occasionally wondered at the bounty of Nature.

Suddenly, my attention went to the narrowness of the path. It was hardly one foot wide but one was able to walk on it comfortably without any insecurity of falling off. Then I thought that while there was no problem in walking on a one foot wide path, the same would become difficult if one had to walk on a one foot wide wall. This difficulty would further increase with the increase in the height of a wall and it would perhaps, become impossible for a common person to walk over even a two feet wide wall, if its height was raised to ten feet or more. The fact is, that one needs the same width even to walk on a wall but the sense of insecurity increases because of the height and makes it difficult to walk. However, a trained and disciplined person could walk even on a rope tied at a great height.

This observation gave me a very valuable lesson for life. As long as we are not very important and remain on the ground, our needs are few and we enjoy life within our limited means. As we grow materially, and reach the so-called height, it becomes difficult to live within the same means while our basic needs remain the same. Not only this, our joys turn into fears, as and when we start possessing more. Our energies are then deployed in acquiring more and the process goes on. In this way, while one's income level increases, his or her happiness decreases.

The answer lies in appreciating the fact that when we rise in life, we need more discipline and restraint for remaining happy. No one can deny that our basic needs of food, shelter and clothing remain the same, but we tend to acquire more only due to our sense of insecurity or ego. A wise person is one, who can correctly assess his needs and spend his energy optimally. His acquisitions beyond his needs then serve a larger purpose and cater to the society. This further adds to his happiness and fulfilment in life. Someone has rightly said that the only way for a rich man to be happy is, to live like a poor man.

*****

Do it with Calm

When I was the principal secretary of an important public utility department, I had a secretary who was a very honest and sincere officer. We both joined the department almost simultaneously, he being only few days senior to me. The department was known for corruption and inefficiency, but to the extent that it was kept a secret for us till we joined the department. My younger friend discovered it soon and was baffled.

Few days after I joined, he gave me a call one evening asking if he could meet me immediately. Incidentally, I was relatively free and had no visitor or officials around. So I asked him to come immediately so that we could talk at ease and he did. His body language revealed discomfort and he appeared to be in a state of confusion. Going by his sincerity and reputation, it was an unusual sight and I also grew curious.

Then he told me about a call which he had received few hours back from a vendor who used to supply posters for a certain health programme. The caller sought instruction from him with regard to his commission, which fell due on account of the last campaign, held soon after he had joined. The amount was about three lakh rupees and the manner and place of payment had also been discussed. This was a situation he had never come across in his career and was confused about his response to such a strange call. He appeared to be quite angry at the vendor and wanted to take strong action against him. He sought my advice in this regard. Set apart the real problem which would be dealt with separately, my immediate concern was his agony. Here was a person who was honest and sincere but was suffering on account of the misdeeds of others. This was the least thing I wanted for him.

With a touch of humour, I then told him that there were only two options before him. Either he calmly accepted the money or calmly refused it. Instead, he was choosing a third option that of refusing the vendor with anger. In this way, he was going to be a double sufferer. He got my point and felt somewhat relaxed. Then we discussed the matter from the administrative point of view. I advised him to understand the whole process and take necessary steps to stop the malpractice for all times to come. I also assured him my full cooperation.

He took my advice seriously and soon worked out a plan, which could address the problem at its root. In the very next campaign, there was a saving of about forty percent, much more than the cut that was being offered to him. Incidentally, the vendor also appreciated his initiative as this removed his dilemma too.

This was possible only because the whole chain of events was carried out with a calm frame of mind.

*****

Breakfast is the Same

I served in the capacity of secretary, medical education twice. In that position, Sanjay Gandhi Post Graduate Institute of Medical Sciences (SGPGI), Lucknow came under my department. This gave me an opportunity to come in contact with several good doctors. The friendship and association with many of them continues till date. One such doctor was several years younger to me. He was known for his competence as well as his manners. Patients felt very comfortable with him and his name spread fast in the medical fraternity. Incidentally, I was also one of his patients and this brought us even closer.

After serving for few years at SGPGI, he got an offer from the Apollo hospital at Delhi. Though he was very happy at Lucknow, he decided to shift mainly on account of some personal problems. He was very well aware of the fact that SGPGI campus at Lucknow provided much more peace than what he would find in Delhi. After shifting to Delhi, he got a residence quite far from his place of work. Travelling to his work place in the morning and back home in the evening consumed about two hours of his. However, from the emoluments point of view, the Delhi job was much better than the Lucknow job.

It was during this period, when I visited him in Delhi. I had gone there for training and was staying at a place very near to his residence. One morning, I fixed up an appointment with him and reached his place half an hour before he used to leave for the hospital. That day, he had some other work also and, therefore, was to leave about fifteen minutes earlier than usual. As a result, he was in a hurry and we could barely exchange pleasantries. During this period, I noticed that he was taking his breakfast – standing with a dry bun in one hand and a cup of coffee in the other.

This looked quite amusing to me and my attention went to those poor people who take the same breakfast but in much more relaxed way and I humorously pointed out this to him. My comparison of his breakfast was with that of a rickshaw-puller of Lucknow who takes his breakfast on a roadside tea stall in a relaxed manner. At that time, he either refuses to attend his customer or makes him wait till he finishes his munch.

My young doctor friend was in total agreement with me but had no alternative. He had come to Delhi for better professional achievement and not for better breakfast. Eventually, he achieved much more name and fame in due course. However, I have no information about his breakfast and whether it continues to be the same or has become even simpler.

*****

When We Think Positive

*M*ata Amritanandamayi is one of the greatest saints in India, who is doing laudable work for the society along with her spiritual pursuits. Her presence is now felt in every part of the world. Going by her background, it is a great wonder that she is serving the society which can be possible only due to divine grace. No wonder she is considered to be an incarnation of God herself. Her affectionate embrace is like a blessing for all those who meet her. The devotees wait for their turn, for hours, while Ma seems to be never getting tired in displaying her affection and with equal intensity from the beginning to the end.

In March 2006, Amma visited Lucknow. A large public appearance was organised for her in an open space. At that time, I was the commissioner of Lucknow and in that capacity, got the privilege of being of some help to this function. It was for the first time that I came in contact with Amma and her entourage. The programme was conducted very gracefully and Ma endeared herself to her audience in Lucknow just like everywhere else.

I wished that Amma could visit my home in Lucknow for a few minutes. When I expressed this wish, I was assured that Amma would try her best to do so and soon it was confirmed that Amma would visit my house in the early hours just after she met and embraced her devotees. My family remained anxious throughout the night and Amma visited our home as per her assurance and spent about half an hour with us. This was a memorable day of our life and we all felt blessed in a true sense. The members of the entourage also invited me to Amma's *ashram* in Kerala.

Amma's main *ashram* is in the Kollam district of Kerala and Amma is available there only for a part of the year and that too, at different times. While I wished to visit her there, looking at the low probability of my being in Kerala during her presence in the *ashram*, I never committed myself to this. But perhaps, Amma was more graceful to me than I could think of.

In April 2009, I visited Kerala during my journey to Lakshadweep, the destination of my LTC (Leave Travel Concession). I was to stay in Lakshadweep for three days, which had to be cut short by one day because of the change in airline schedule. As a result, I got one day extra at Cochin. As I was heading towards the town from the Airport on 25th April, I got a call from Lucknow and Amma's reference was made. Immediately, I noticed a hoarding for Amma's programme. This created a desire in me to pay her my tribute, if possible.

Soon, I contacted some of my local friends who told me that Amma was in her *ashram* but having come there after a long time, it was very difficult to meet her. Somehow, my urge was deep and I decided to visit the *ashram* even if meeting Amma was not possible. Deep within my heart, I was positive and hopeful. As we reached the *ashram*, we were received very warmly by some devotees who were also trying to arrange my meeting with Amma against all hopes. Eventually, a message came from her and I along with my local friends were called in her living room and given an audience for almost 30 minutes, a privilege rarely available to anyone. For me, it was an indication of Amma's grace and the power of my positive thinking that helped me meet her.

*****